SEWING

ALTERATIONS & REPAIRS

200 QUESTIONS ANSWERED

Questions answered on everything from mending to makeovers

Nan Ides

Search Press

Forever thank you to my grandmother, who had the patience to continue the wonderful and inspirational tradition of sewing

A Quantum Book

Published in 2011 by Search Press Ltd.
Wellwood, North Farm Road,
Tunbridge Wells,
Kent TN2 3DR

This book is produced by
Quantum Publishing
6 Blundell Street
London
N7 9BH

ISBN: 978-1-84448-759-2

QUM2QAS

Publisher: Sarah Bloxham
Managing Editor: Julie Brooke
Editor: Caroline Smith
Project Editor: Samantha Warrington
Assistant Editor: Jo Morley
Design: Dave Jones
Photographer: Marcos Bevilacqua
Production: Rohana Yusof

Printed in China by
Midas Printing International Ltd.

CONTENTS

Introduction 6

Chapter 1: What Is This Book All About? 8
Chapter 2: Basic Tools and Techniques 20
Chapter 3: Buttons, Zips and Other Closures 54
Chapter 4: Hand Mending Know-How 82
Chapter 5: Machine-Sewing Know-How 108
Chapter 6: Ironing and Pressing 122
Chapter 7: Altering Skirts and Trousers to Fit 134
Chapter 8: Altering Tops, Dresses and Jackets to Fit 150
Chapter 9: Altering the Style of Clothing 174
Chapter 10: Adapting Bargains and Other Money-Saving Ideas 192
Chapter 11: Taking Your Sewing Skills Further 206

Index 222
Acknowledgments 224

INTRODUCTION

When I was contacted to write this book I was excited and incredibly honoured. And then panic set in: I was going to have to write about a topic that I could literally talk about for days, weeks, even months. There is so much to say! Learning to mend and sew can open up a whole new world. For me, it's like walking into a library full of millions of books; so much information and so much to learn!

I have known how to mend my entire life. My grandparents were dressmakers and a sewing basket and sewing machine were always ready for use at their home and mine. Also, my family are quite short (I am 5 feet, and shrinking) and when I was younger, ranges of petite clothing hadn't come in yet. All shop-bought clothes had to be altered in some way – sleeves shortened and shoulders taken in; dresses, trousers and skirts hemmed.

As the middle child of three girls, I didn't get many new clothes when I was growing up. I received hand-me-downs from my older sister or cousins. These clothes were taken in for one person; taken out for the next; hemmed up; hemmed down with added trims; repaired and so on. You made do with what you had and then passed them on to the next relative until the clothes could not be worn anymore. Then you donated them or they became rags for cleaning; no one 'threw' clothing away. At a time when charity shops didn't have much to choose from and designer outlets were unheard of, this was how almost everyone lived.

When I graduated from college in the early 1980s and began my first 'real' jobs, I thought being a more mature professional would mean buying store-bought clothes and getting them professionally altered. After a while, I had some lovely professionally altered, store-bought clothes, but no money! Not only was I paying more for my clothes, I was paying again to have them altered to fit. I soon realised that it would be more mature to save my money by altering things myself.

I am a huge fan of charity shops and dress exchanges. In the 1980s, these types of outlet were really starting to become popular. Recycling was back in style and I was loving it! I began to get a bit more creative – purchasing new styles, 'funky' clothes and home decorations to experiment with and possibly rip apart and redo. I was paying so little, that I never felt that I was wasting money. (Although, over the years it has become quite addictive!)

I usually never go into charity shops or dress exchanges with just one thing in mind that I need to purchase. I look through the whole store, even going through the garments in other sizes – you never know what you will find that can be easily altered. I also like to look for unique items or something a little different than I usually wear, just to try out the new style. Wherever I go in the world, I try to find similar stores (I actually bought a second-hand silk kimono in a shop in Japan!).

It doesn't take involved sewing skills to mend and alter, or even to experiment a little. It just takes some basic skills and a little creativity. Once you've learnt the simple techniques needed, you'll find there's no stopping you! Go through your wardrobe or simply walk around your house. Do you have clothes that have been sitting in your cupboards for over a year? Are the buttons missing, are they too long, is the zipper broken? Gather everything into a pile, have this book close by and begin! I will bet that within a few hours, you will have several new garments to wear. Not only will you have saved yourself some money, you will also have done your bit towards recycling clothing. And you'll be having fun at the same time!

I'd like to take this opportunity to thank my good friends Pamela Leggett and Jacqueline Fowlkes for their help in making the sewn samples for this book. And thanks too to Pati Palmer, of Palmer Pletsch, who took a chance with me and published my first mending book.

When you are mending or altering your clothes, you will want your finished work to be more-or-less invisible – unless, of course, you're adding a decorative touch! So you'll need to use matching thread and make small, unobtrusive stitches.

However, to make sure that the stitching shown in some of the pictures in this book is easy to see, the sewing has been done with a strongly coloured thread. Also, to make sure that some of the alterations are visible, seams, hems and darts have been made wider than they would be in reality for clarity's sake.

1. What is the difference between mending and altering a garment?
2. What kind of mending techniques will I learn?
3. What kind of alterations will I be able to do?
4. How can mending techniques help me save money?
5. Isn't it easier to get a local tailor to make alterations?
6. What does it take to learn to hand mend?
7. Are there other benefits to learning to hand mend?
8. What does the term 'ready-made clothes' refer to?
9. What is the ideal age to start teaching children simple sewing?
10. What would be good sewing projects for children to begin learning?

1

WHAT IS THIS BOOK ALL ABOUT?

Question 1:
What is the difference between mending and altering a garment?

Hand mending is the act of fixing something that has ripped or has torn, such as sewing a button back on, stitching a ripped seam, patching a torn knee on your child's jeans or even fixing a zip that is stuck. Hand mending is just that, usually done by hand (of course, some mending can be done with the sewing machine, but this is usually not necessary).

Alterations are usually done with a sewing machine. The alterations, as presented in this book, are for changing and making ready-made garments look better fitted and more stylish – to look as if the clothes were made just for you and to add some creativity and flair. Alterations could be anything, such as taking in the side seams of a blazer to make it look more flattering, taking up the shoulders of a garment so it is more fitted, or shortening those curtains that would be perfect for your guest room.

EXPERT TIP

“ If you take up sewing, you'll be taking up a craft that is millenia old. Hand sewing has been around for more than twenty thousand years. The first sewing needles were made of slivers of bone or animal horn and the first thread was animal sinew. Iron needles were invented in the fourteenth century, although they didn't have eyes until the fifteenth century. ”

ABOVE Sewing is a satisfying and rewarding pastime. Learn to sew and you'll have the skills to repair and refashion your wardrobe.

Question 2:
What kind of mending techniques will I learn?

In this book, you will start off with the really basic basics. You'll learn how to thread a needle, and how to knot the thread and start stitching. You'll find out how to sew on different types of buttons, press studs, and hooks and eyes – even how to create a thread-chain eye for a hook. You'll discover how to fix a stuck zip, mend a ripped seam, patch a tear on trousers or elbows, and fix those little pulls in your favourite sweater. You'll even learn how to hem your daughter's jeans to stop them dragging on the ground! After learning the basic mending and sewing skills, you should be able to fix or mend almost anything.

Question 3:
What kind of alterations will I be able to do?

Alterations are a little more involved, but not necessarily more difficult. Alterations could be anything from taking in the side seams of a shirt to fit your curves better and make it look more flattering; hemming jeans and keeping the faded, washed-out original hem; taking up the shoulders of a top so it fits better and doesn't look too big, even if the rest of the blouse fits well; shortening those curtains that you want to move to a different room, even adding some lace or trim to those curtains. You will also learn how to put elastic in to the waistband of trousers, lengthen your children's clothes as they grow and even transform that old but cherished stained tablecloth.

Question 4:
How can mending techniques help me save money?

By learning to mend, you will no longer need to take small sewing jobs to the tailor. Take a look at the chart below to see how much you could actually save. A tailor will charge you good money to sew on a button when you could do this yourself in less than 5 minutes. Add to this the cost of travelling to get to the tailor and back again, not to mention the time you've taken.

Alteration to be done	Fee charged by tailor
Shortening trousers	£10–12
Tapering trouser legs	£15–25
Repairing trouser pockets	£12–15
Shortening a skirt	£10–12
Taking in a skirt	£14–£15
Shortening sleeves	£12–£15
Shortening cuffed sleeves	£14–£18
Sewing on buttons	£1.50 each
Replacing & sewing on buttons	£1.50 each (plus cost of button)
Ripped seams	from £15 depending on size & location of rip
Sewing on patches	£5–£7

Question 5:
Isn't it easier to get a local tailor to make alterations?

While it may be easier to take something to a tailor and have them do alterations, in the long run, it is easier and more economical for you to learn yourself. Yes, there will still be times when it may be more logical to have an experienced tailor alter a garment (for example, when replacing a zip, taking up the shoulders, hemming pleated shirts, or if something has to be done in a rush). But think about the time it takes to gather up the garment, drive to the tailors, the money to pay them and then pick up the garment when it is done. Wouldn't it be easier to learn to sew that button on yourself? Why buy a great bargain at a charity shop or discount store, if you are going take it to the tailor's and spend the money you just saved?

ABOVE A tailor may be an option if you need to make a significant alteration or repair to a complex garment such as a suit jacket.

Question 6:
What does it take to learn to hand mend?

I tell everyone I teach that anyone can learn to hand mend. I have had students of all ages – boys, girls, men and women – in my classes. At one time, I had a class with six widowers who were tired of paying the tailor to sew back on the little tiny clear plastic buttons from their tailored shirts. In one hour, I taught them not only how to sew the buttons on, but many other skills as well. They were thrilled. Not only were they going to save money, they did not feel as 'lost' without their wives and so much more confident of their capabilities to continue living alone. That's why learning simple skills can help anyone – going off to college, joining the military, going camping, even getting married.

So, what does it take to learn to hand mend? Some simple mending supplies, a little patience and practice, just like anything new. No one is perfect, not even the most experienced designer or tailor, but with practice you will get better and better and much more confident and able to do more and more involved alterations. Pretty soon you will be using your skills to create your own clothing styles and decorate your home!

LEFT You can start learning sewing skills with just a few very basic supplies.

Question 7:
Are there other benefits to learning to hand mend?

Hand mending is a very important skill to acquire if you wish to keep your clothes in better shape and for longer. Many benefits to learning mending and sewing skills have been mentioned, such as saving money, saving time, confidence building and so much more. With a few basic sewing skills, you could create wonderful hand-made gifts, such as placemats and stuffed toys.

Yes, you can certainly take these items needing to be fixed to a tailor, however, why waste that money when you can do it yourself with a few easy lessons.

Question 8:
What does the term 'ready-made clothes' refer to?

Ready-made garments are the mass-produced finished products of the clothing industry. In other words, they are any clothes that you buy in a store that are not hand-made, specially ordered or personalised for you. Almost all the alterations and repairs discussed in this book will be done to ready-made garments.

ABOVE You can use your new skills to transform ready-made clothes.

Question 9:
What is the ideal age to start teaching children simple sewing?

I was fortunate enough to grow up in a house where there was always a sewing box and sewing machine somewhere. And because my family is petite, almost all of our purchased clothes needed to be altered or at least shortened – even sleeves, pants, etc. So our family all learned mending and altering skills at an early age.

There's no hard-and-fast rules as to what age a child should begin sewing. As long as they have enough manual dexterity and coordination to be able to hold a large (children's plastic) needle, they can learn. This usually means that they are already writing, drawing and/or colouring in by themselves.

They should be coordinated enough (after a few tries – remember it's a new skill and they will need to practise) to push a needle in and pull it out of a piece of fabric. And most importantly, not to use the needle (plastic or otherwise) as a weapon!

Most sewing stores have some type of children's kit, usually a larger, plastic needle to use with some yarn to get used to the idea of a real needle. Failing that, let them use a large, blunt metal needle, the type used for tapestry.

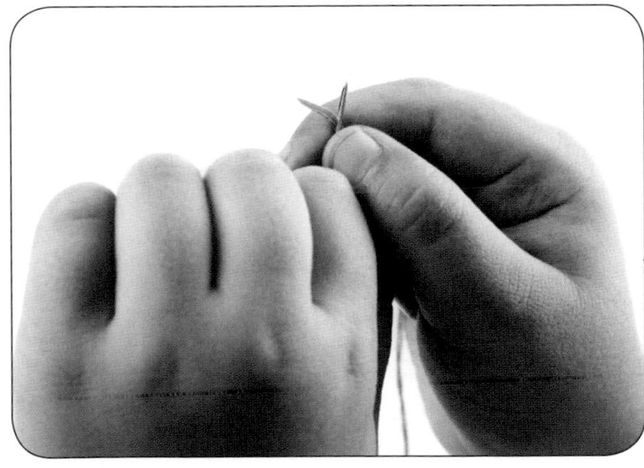

LEFT Even little hands can handle a needle and thread.

Question 10:
What would be good sewing projects for children to begin learning?

It's a good idea to use children's utensils. The plastic canvas needlework kits with large holes, a large plastic needle and yarn make wonderful learning tools. Usually a very simple picture has been printed on to the canvas and the child can learn needle coordination, as well as how to follow simple instructions, even if they cannot read themselves.

- Threading the needle is the most basic function involved with sewing and should be the first skill learned by all beginners. To practise threading the needle, the beginner should hold it in one hand, perpendicular to the ground. In the other hand, he should hold the end of the thread. The child can lick the thread to make it more rigid. Have him feed the thread through the eye. Once the thread is through the needle you can take the thread out and keep practising.

- Knotting the thread, which takes more coordination, may be difficult for a younger child and possibly an adult should do that. However, if the child seems able, have them lay the threaded needle on a hard surface and make a knot using both hands. Then, pull the thread through. It will take a few practise tries to get the knot toward the end of the thread. Now is not the time to expect perfection!

- Practise sewing straight lines by hand. Draw a few straight lines on a piece of fabric a few inches apart. With a threaded needle, have the child push the needle up through the wrong side of the fabric and through to the right side on the drawn line. The thread should be pulled tight, but not too tight. The child should then push the needle down through the fabric along the same line a couple of centimetres away and pull the thread tight. Repeat this process until they are at the end of the line and bring the needle up to the next row. Practise keeping each stitch no longer than 2.5cm (1in) and about the same size throughout.

ABOVE Once a child has had a bit of practice making hand stitches, you can – carefully – introduce them to the sewing machine.

11 What are some of the important mending terms I should know?

12 What are the most basic supplies necessary for hand mending?

13 Are there any useful 'extras' that would make mending easier?

14 Do I need to spend a lot on special supplies and where can I purchase such items?

15 Why are there so many different types of straight pins?

16 How many pairs of scissors should I have?

17 Do I need a sewing machine?

18 When should I use a sewing machine as opposed to sewing by hand?

19 How do I thread a needle?

20 What is a needle-threader?

21 How and when would I use a needle-threader?

22 What is the ideal way to hold a needle when sewing?

23 What type or size of needle should I use for hand mending?

24 What are the different types of threads?

25 Do I need all these different types of thread?

26 How do I know what type of thread to use for my project?

27 What are the best basic colours and lengths of thread to have available?

28 I don't have the exact colour thread; what is my next choice?

29 How long should the thread be for hand mending?

30 When do I need to use thread doubled?

31 How do I knot the thread?

32 How do I secure my stitches to begin?

33 How do I end the stitching?

34 What does 'rip out' mean?

35 What is the best tool to use for ripping out?

36 What is an overlocker?

37 What is topstitching?

38 What are the basic sewing stitches that would be most useful?

39 What is tacking stitch and how do I do it?

40 What is hemming stitch and how do I do it?

41 What is catch stitch and how do I do it?

42 What is slip stitch and how do I do it?

43 What is backstitch and how do I do it?

44 What is overcast or blanket stitch and how do I do it?

2

BASIC TOOLS AND TECHNIQUES

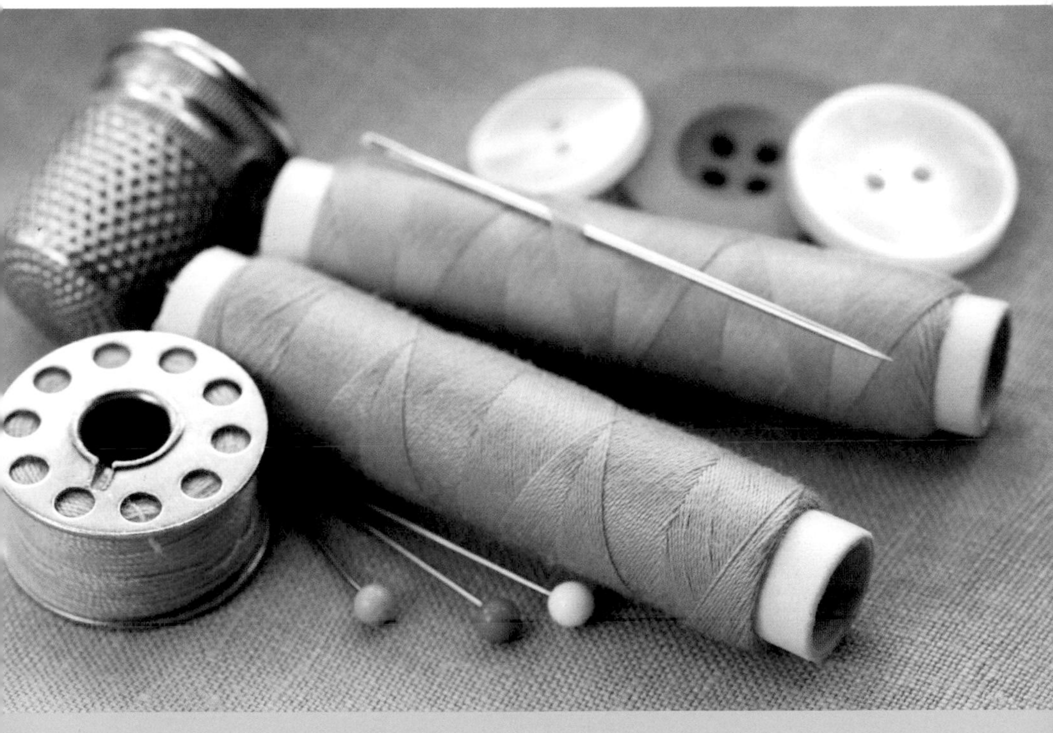

Question 11:
What are some of the important mending terms I should know?

There are lots of different terms used in sewing and you won't need to know every single technical term to be able to mend and alter your clothes. However, there are few terms that are worth noting.

- Hemming finishes the raw edge of a garment so that it won't rip or fray. This is typically done by folding the edge over once or twice, and then sewing it down. Hemming is used to change the length of a garment.
- The eye of the needle is the hole at the end of the needle where the thread goes through.
- The right side of the fabric is the side that will show on the outside of a garment. The wrong side of the fabric is the inside.
- Seam allowances are the area of fabric between the raw edge of a seam and the stitching line.
- Wovens are non–stretch fabrics (although there are exceptions, especially with materials such as spandex being incorporated in man-made fabrics).
- Knits are fabrics that stretches either two ways (horizontally) or four ways (stretching both horizontally and vertically).
- Spandex is a man-made fibre that adds stretch and which is always blended with other fibres (such as to add some stretch to jeans). Spandex improves the fit and flexibility of a garment, while enhancing durability. Lycra, a registered trademark of DuPont, is one of the most popular brands of spandex.

ABOVE On printed fabrics, the wrong side of the material is obvious; the pattern will be indistinct when compared to the right side.

Question 12:
What are the most basic supplies necessary for hand mending?

ABOVE You can keep your sewing supplies in any box you choose; just make sure it's big enough to hold everything you need.

The supplies that are absolutely necessary to hand mend garments and other things are few and inexpensive. However, it must be noted that a huge industry has been created that manufactures every conceivable kind of sewing item. Are all of these supplies necessary? Of course not, however many will make your mending and sewing much easier. Basic supplies include several needles, several spools of different colour threads, some straight pins, several safety pins, and at least one of the following: a cutting utensil (scissors that can cut fabric or a rotary cutter), a measuring utensil (a tape measure and ruler), and a marking utensil (tailor's chalk, disappearing marking pen). And not forgetting some reading glasses!

Question 13:
Are there any useful 'extras' that would make mending easier?

The answer to this question is a resounding 'yes', but as stated in Question 12, most are not necessary, they are just helpful. A few of those extras which I find to be extremely helpful are: a full-length mirror; a pin cushion; some tailor's chalk; beeswax (this helps thread slide through the fabric more easily); a rotary cutter; a seam ripper; some Fray Check (similar to a clear nail varnish, this doesn't dry hard and stops fabrics fraying); a needle threader (see Questions 20 and 21); a magnetic pin holder; extra buttons; extra needles; and safety pins. There are so many other items on the market that are useful, such as: thimbles; hem gauge (a little gadget to help ensure even hem lengths); embroidery needles; disappearing marker pens; rolling chalk wheels; fusible hemming tape; and an elastic bodkin.

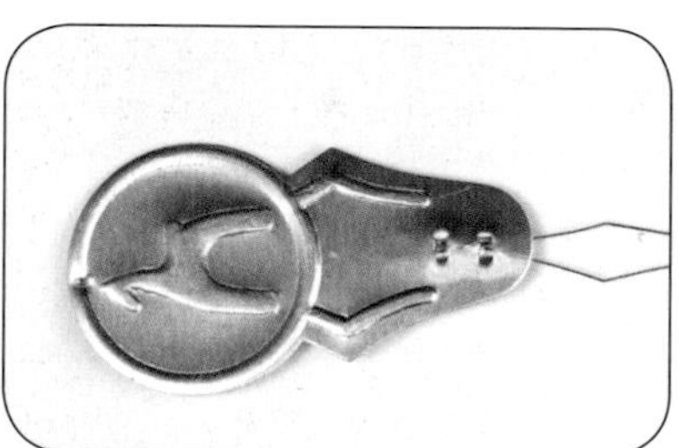

ABOVE A needle threader.

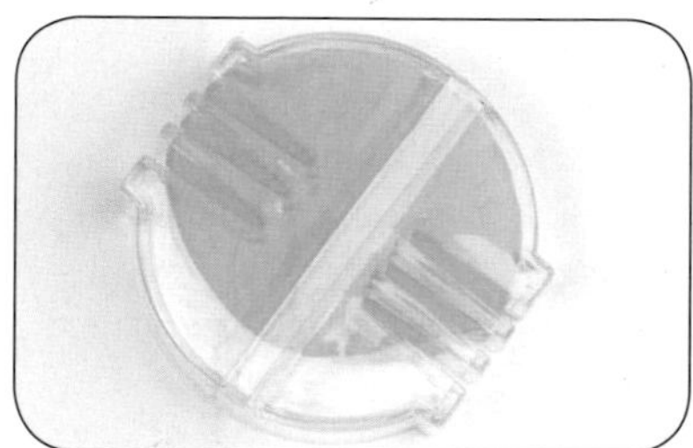

ABOVE Beeswax, to rub on thread.

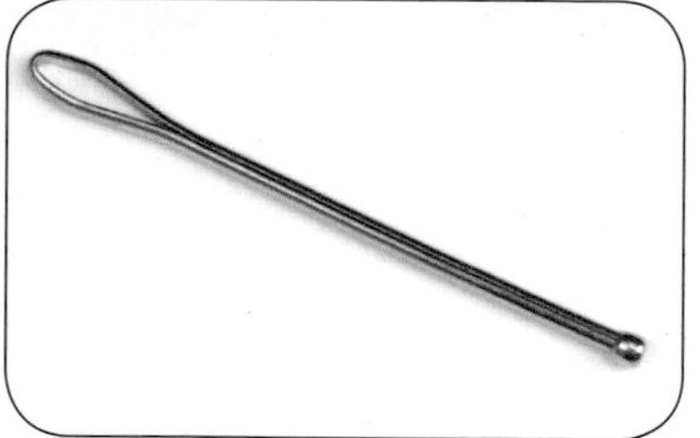

ABOVE A bodkin, for threading elastic.

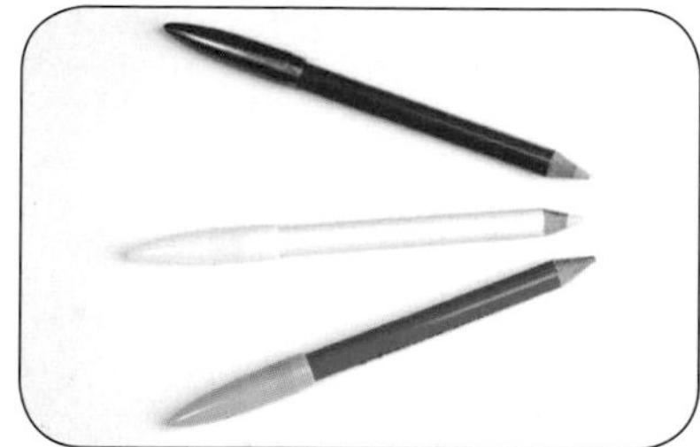

ABOVE Tailor's chalk in pencil form.

Question 14:
Do I need to spend a lot on special supplies and where can I purchase such items?

For very basic supplies, you do not need to spend a lot of money. Some stores sell very basic mending kits, containing inexpensive items such as needles, a few straight pins, extra buttons, a few colours of thread and a needle or two. However, the thread in these kits should only be used for emergencies because it will break very easily.

Sewing and craft stores usually have the best selection of items and just like any other hobby, you can spend hours trying to figure out if you actually need those 'helpful items'. My suggestion is to walk around these shops and see what types of items are available and what each item is used for. Then, start with some good quality basics and see if you really need all of those 'extras'.

EXPERT TIP

“ Often, when you buy blouses, jackets, coats, and even pyjama tops, spare buttons are often attached to the garment. Don't throw these away; keep them safe in your button tin. Even if you never need them for the garment in question, you may well find them useful for other projects. ”

Question 15:
Why are there so many different types of straight pins?

Straight pins (as opposed to safety pins) vary in length, thickness, type of head and in the type of point at the tip. They are usually made of steel, but sometimes brass or nickel pins are found. Nickel-plating helps prevent steel pins from rusting.

Typical sewing pins have flat metal heads and are called, unsurprisingly, flat pins. You'll also find pins with ball-shaped heads, usually made of coloured glass or plastic, and these are known as ball pins. The advantage of this type of pin is that they are easier to see and to pick up. There are also pins with T-shaped heads – known as T pins – that are ideal for use with very open weaves since the head won't slip through the weave.

Ordinary straight pins are fine for most sewing jobs that you will be doing. However, you may consider buying specialist pins when working with certain fabrics. If you're using a knit type of fabric, for example, try T pins with blunt points (known as ball points); the rounded points will slip between the fibres of the fabric and the T head will keep the pins secure. On delicate silks, use the finest pins available, with the sharpest points, so you avoid leaving holes in the fabric.

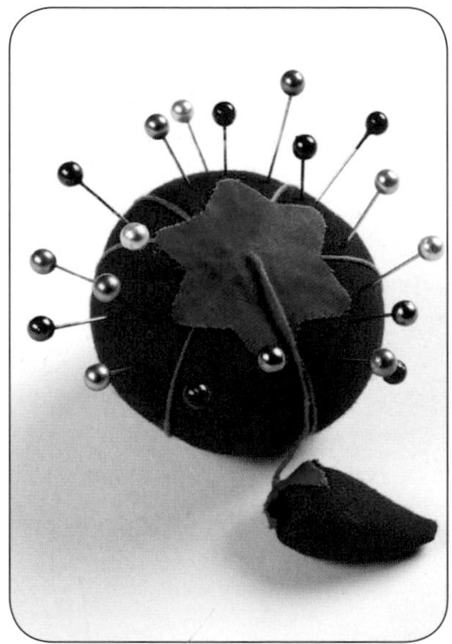

ABOVE If you keep your pins in a pin cushion, the points stay sharper longer.

Question 16:
How many pairs of scissors should I have?

For the most basic sewing jobs you really only need one pair of scissors. These should be a good quality pair that you can use for cutting both fabric and thread. Dressmaking shears are ideal; they are distinguished from ordinary household scissors by handles that bend upwards – this allows fabric to lie flat when being cut. If you invest in a decent pair, they should last a lifetime. Just remember to keep them for sewing use only; use them for other tasks and they'll blunt very quickly.

Small, embroidery scissors can be very useful, especially when hand mending. The small, thin blades are useful for ripping out stitches and cutting away small, fiddly areas. It may also be worth investing in pinking shears too. These heavy-duty scissors cut a zigzag edge that is particularly useful for finishing the raw edges of fabric or for cutting a decorative edge.

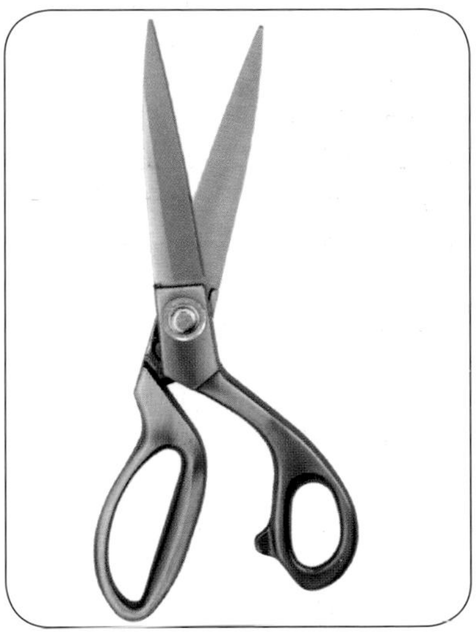

ABOVE Dressmaking shears are the ideal scissors for cutting fabric.

Question 17:
Do I need a sewing machine?

This book is divided into two skill areas – mending that is sewn by hand, and simple repairs and alterations done with a sewing machine.

For the hand-mending skills covered in this book, you will not need to use a sewing machine. All the skills you'll learn will be done with a simple needle and thread. However, beginning with Chapter 5, this book will cover other fixes and alterations that might need the use of a sewing machine combined with some basic machine stitches. So if you don't have a sewing machine, it is well worth considering buying one. You'll find you are able to do so much more than if you rely solely on hand sewing. And who knows how much further you will want to take things, once you've taken up such a rewarding hobby.

ABOVE A good-quality sewing machine that does all the stitches you need shouldn't be too expensive; you can find a decent model for around £100.

Question 18:

When should I use a sewing machine as opposed to sewing by hand?

A long time ago, before sewing machines were invented, people sewed all their clothes, linens and furnishings by hand. As a consequence, the standard of hand sewing was extremely high. Now, only the very top European couture designer houses still sew clothes by hand because of the detail, skill and time it takes. Couture refers to that part of the fashion industry devoted to producing top designs made to an exceptional standard. The word is French for sewing; 'haute couture' means 'high sewing' and thus is used to denote those fashion houses or designers that specialise in custom-made garments for specific customers. Haute couture clothes are made from high-quality, designer fabrics and constructed with intricate detail from start to finish.

Once you have mastered the basic sewing skills, it will be up to you as to where and when you choose to sew by hand and or machine. It will also depend on what needs to be fixed or altered. This will be a question that you will need to answer yourself. Of course, there are things that cannot be done by machine – sewing on buttons, press studs and hooks, for example – and there are things that are not practical and too time consuming if they are done by hand – such as stitching long seams, sewing in elastic and making darts.

Question 19:
How do I thread a needle?

Threading a needle is the first step to learning how to mend. Hold the thread between the thumb and forefinger about 5–10mm (¼–½in) away from the end of the thread. If you hold the thread inches away from the end, the thread will just flop down. Sometimes dampening the thread (with the tip of your tongue or between the lips) helps stabilise it. Simply push the thread through the eye of the needle. Practise using a needle with a larger eye; embroidery needles are thicker and have larger eyes intended for thicker yarns and embroidery thread. After practising, try threading smaller eyed needles. When you are ready to start sewing, use a smaller thinner needle that will glide through the fabric easily and not leave marks.

EXPERT TIP

“When threading the needle, you can also try closing one eye. This helps because the vision balancing is done for you. You can try bringing the needle toward the thread as opposed to trying to push the thread into the needle eye; it may work better. Another idea that may help is to hold the eye of the needle in front of a white background. You can always try a needle-threader too; see Questions 20 and 21.”

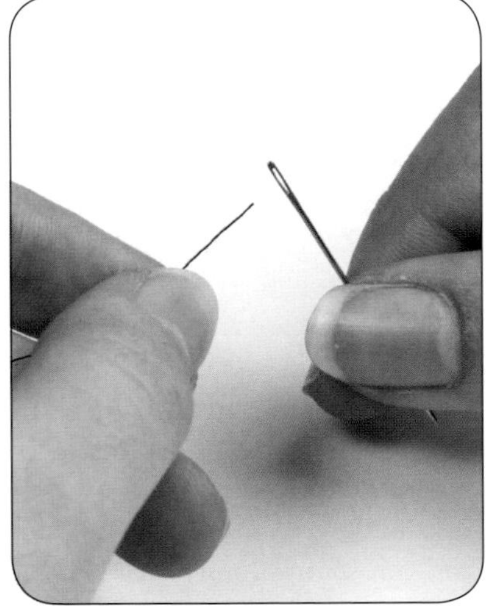

ABOVE Hold the needle steady in whichever hand feels most comfortable. Then simply push the end of the thread into the eye.

Question 20:
What is a needle-threader?

A needle-threader is a very inexpensive, small tool that helps thread the needle when you are having problems seeing the eye of the needle (see Question 13).

A piece of wire, bent into a diamond shape, is mounted in a thin, shaped piece of light metal. You can push the point of the wire into the eye of the needle.

Question 21:
How and when would I use a needle-threader?

You can use a needle-threader anytime you wish. You do not have to be far-sighted (you can't see close-up things and need reading glasses) to have trouble threading a needle; the eyes are small, after all. You can also use a needle-threader to thread a sewing machine needle (although many sewing machines have built-in needle threaders).

Push the wire loop of the threader through the eye of the needle. Slip your thread into the wire loop. Pull the loop back through the eye of the needle, pulling the thread with it.

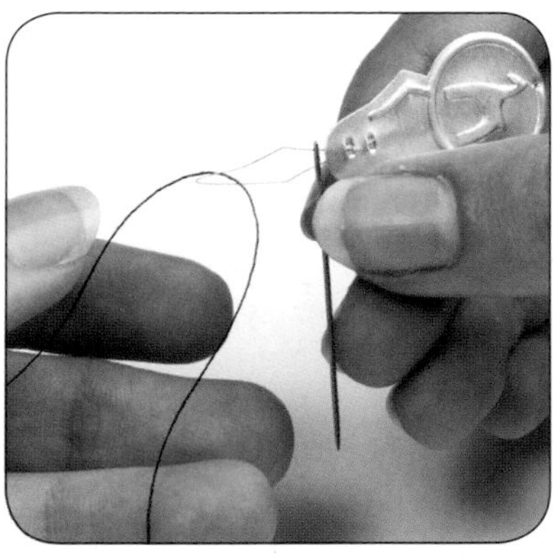

ABOVE Once you've pushed the threader through the eye of the needle, slip your thread into the wire loop. Pull the threader out to draw the thread through the needle.

Question 22:
What is the ideal way to hold a needle when sewing?

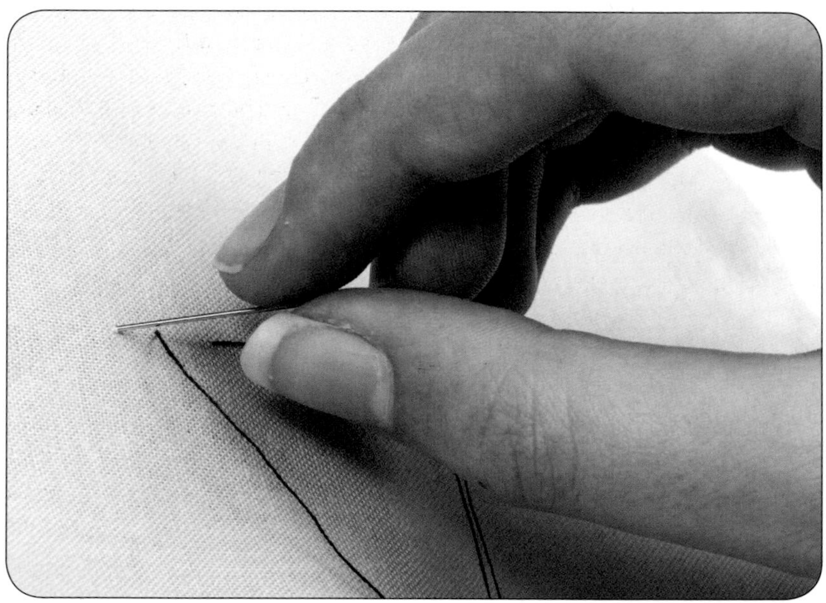

ABOVE Hold the needle between your thumb and forefinger, and use the middle finger to push the blunt end of the needle.

Holding a needle may feel uncomfortable at first, just like learning to hold a pencil, or a knife and fork, or even chopsticks. But with practise, it will soon come naturally. Hold the needle between your thumb and forefinger and using your middle finger, push the needle through the fabric. The thumb and middle finger should be placed on the eye of the needle to prevent the thread from slipping out as you sew. Hold the fabric over the index finger of the other hand with your thumb on top. Usually, right-handed people hand sew from right to left and left-handed people hand sew from left to right, however do what is most comfortable for you.

Question 23:
What type or size of needle should I use for hand mending?

Needles come in different lengths, widths and with different sizes of eyes. Some people recommend using the smallest needle possible – and of course, the smaller the needle, the smaller the eye you have to thread! However, average-size needles will be fine for most mending jobs. My suggestion is to buy a pack of different size needles and see which are more comfortable for you. As the needle gets thinner and the eye get smaller, the needle also gets shorter. If you have small hands, this may be fine, but with larger hands, a longer needle may be more comfortable.

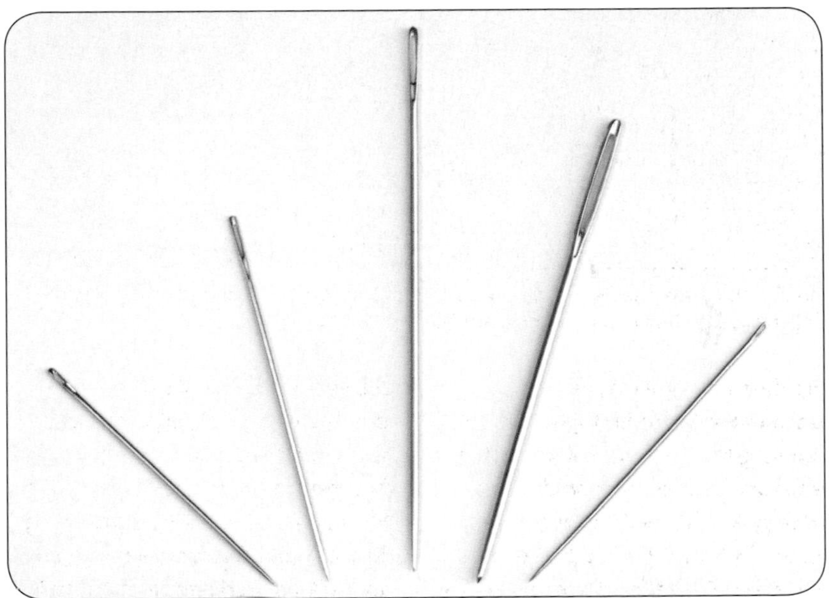

ABOVE Needles come in many different sizes; the narrower the needle, the finer the eye. Blunt needles, used for needlepoint, are useful for mending knits.

Question 24:
What are the different types of threads?

Sewing thread is made from a variety of different fibres. Thread made from 100% cotton is usually mercerised; this is a process that gives the thread a more even surface and that allows the thread to absorb dye more effectively. Cotton thread does not have much stretch in it, so it's not a good choice for using with knits or jersey on a sewing machine.

Thread made from silk is fine yet strong, and has good elasticity, making it ideal for sewing on silk and wool. It's a good, albeit expensive, choice for a tacking thread; it's so fine it won't leave holes from stitching or imprints after pressing.

For sewing light- to medium-weight synthetics, you can use nylon thread, a suitably fine and strong thread. Polyester thread is ideal for woven synthetics, but it is also suitable for sewing on most fabrics, including knits and other stretch fabrics made of any fibre. Most good-quality polyester thread has a finish to it that is designed to let the thread slip easily between the fibres of the fabric being sewn.

You will also find cotton-wrapped polyester thread, an all-purpose thread suitable for most fabrics. It has a strong, elastic polyester core. The cotton wrapped around the core makes the thread more resistant to heat than 100% polyester would be.

You can also get specialist heavy-duty threads for topstitching and sewing heavier fabrics like denim.

Question 25:
Do I need all these different types of thread?

If you are going to do simple mending, you will not need all of these different types of thread. For beginners, I recommend that people buy an inexpensive sewing kit, with about five or six small spools of basic sewing thread, scissors, some needles, a few safety pins, straight pins, a measuring tool and maybe some other extras. The more sewing you do, the more and better supplies you will want to have.

Cheap thread is useful for emergencies but for anything that will be permanent – such as hemming and mending rips in seams – you should buy better quality thread. Cotton-wrapped polyester is inexpensive and will pretty much hold up as long as the garment lasts.

Once you get into more involved sewing, you can begin to buy the better fabric specialty threads – silk for silk fabrics, for example, or topstitching thread for jeans.

ABOVE You can buy thread in a range of different colours. But to start with, you'll need only a basic selection of shades.

Question 26:
How do I know what type of thread to use for my project?

There are speciality threads for every type of fabric and for all manner of projects: for example, if you are sewing silk, you can buy silk thread; if you are making a quilt, you can use quilting thread. But for most basic sewing – and certainly for most mending jobs and simple alterations – a good quality, all-purpose thread will suffice.

There are a number of brands on the market – such as Coats or Gutterman, to name but two – and if you are shopping in a reputable store then whatever brand they favour will be fine for all-purpose sewing. You can also buy sewing thread online, and if you are planning on doing a lot of sewing, this can be more economical since you can buy larger sized reels of thread. However, if you need to get a thread to match to a particular project, then you should visit a store and take that garment with you; you will be much more likely to find the right colour thread this way.

Avoid using cheap thread though. It will not be a good enough quality and may actually damage your sewing machine.

ABOVE Stores sell a wide range of threads. If you are buying thread for a specific item, remember to take it with you to get the colour match right.

Question 27:
What are the best basic colours and lengths of thread to have available?

If your goal is simple mending, you need only a few spools of thread in the most basic colours – black, white, red, blue, maybe brown, and green. If you will be doing more involved mending and machine sewing, start picking up more colours. For most colours, the smaller spools of thread – 100m (110yd) – will be fine. Sometimes, even smaller spools will be sold in 'starter' kits. It often makes more economic sense to buy the larger spools (500m (547yd)) of white and black, since these seem to be the most commonly used colours.

ABOVE You need buy only a few basic colours when you stock your first sewing box.

Question 28:
I don't have the exact colour thread; what is my next choice?

If you are just beginning to hand mend or sew with a machine, you are not going to have, nor will you need, the exact colours to match every fabric. If you can't get the perfect match for your fabric, then it is recommended that you select thread which is one or two shades darker than the fabric in order for it to blend in better. Stitches made in a lighter shade of thread will stand out more.

If the fabric is a plaid or multi-colour print, select that colour which is most dominant to match. If you are sewing on a sewing machine, the same rules apply.

ABOVE If you can't get the absolute perfect match, then choose a thread that is a shade or two darker than the fabric.

Question 29: How long should the thread be for hand mending?

When hand mending, it is recommended that you use thread that is 45–50cm (18–20in) long, no longer. This also applies if you are using a doubled thread; you should cut the thread to 90–100cm (36–40in) long, then when doubled over in the needle, it will be the required length.

As you sew, your thread will fray and twist slightly each time it passes through the fabric. Therefore, the longer the piece of thread you use, the more times it will go through the fabric as you sew. And therefore, it will fray and twist even more. This weakens the thread, making it more liable to snap during sewing or, even worse, after the sewing is finished.

Also, keeping the thread to this length is much easier and more manageable and there is less chance that the thread will become knotted or catch on to something.

If you do sew with an over-long thread, you will notice that as it twists, it rolls up along the length. The thread is just following its natural inclination to twist together. If this happens, you will find a knot forming as you pull the thread through and you won't be able to stitch any further. You will have to cut off the thread, finish it off and start again; an annoying and time-consuming process.

Question 30:
When do I need to use thread doubled?

Whenever you are doing a sewing job and you need a thread with more strength, then this is the time that you should work with a double thread. Situations where this might arise include sewing on buttons, press studs, and hooks and eyes. In other words, it's a good idea to add strength to your stitching when attaching any closure that might take a lot of wear. You could also use a double thread if you're mending a seam that takes a lot of stress, at the underarm for instance.

You can also double the thread for decorative purposes. Using two, or even more, lengths of thread will ensure that the stitching really stands out rather than being hidden. When you're using blanket stitching, for example, a double thread draws attention to the decorative nature of this practical stitch (see Question 44). For hemming and fixing seams where you want the stitching to be hidden, then a single thread should be used.

To work with the thread doubled, cut a 90–100cm (36–40in) length. Thread the needle and then pull the thread down so that both ends of the thread are even at the end. Knot both ends of the thread together before you start sewing.

Question 31: How do I knot the thread?

After threading the needle, take the end of the thread between your thumb and forefinger. (If you are using single thread, just knot one end of the thread. If using double thread, take the two ends of the thread together.) Wrap the thread loosely around your forefinger, keeping the thread in place with your thumb. Sometimes, dampening the forefinger can help. While holding the other end of the thread taut, slide your forefinger back along your thumb, twisting the threads together until the loop that is formed is pushed off the finger. A loose knot should appear at the end of the thread. Pull at the knot to make it tighter. If the thread pulls off your finger without making a knot, try again. Once you have it, you have it.

Another, more elementary way to knot the thread (suggested for children) is to lay the thread on a hard surface and place the thread in a small circle. If using single thread, this can be done before threading the needle; if using double thread, this should be done after threading the needle. Take one end of the thread (or both ends together if using double thread) and pull it through the circle. Keep pulling. As the loop (which becomes the knot) gets smaller, push the knot toward the end of the thread.

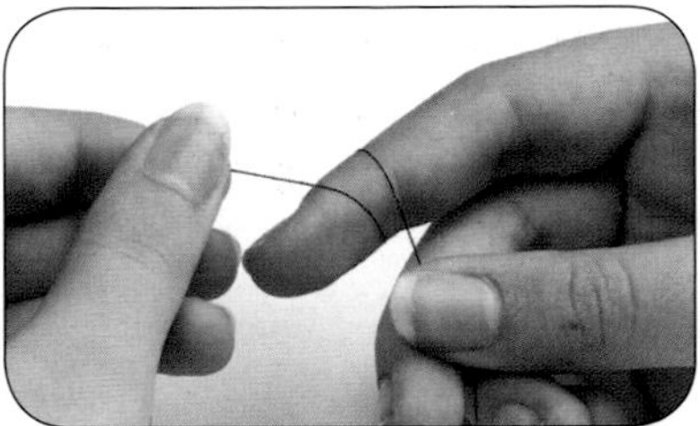

ABOVE Wrap the thread round your forefinger to make a loop.

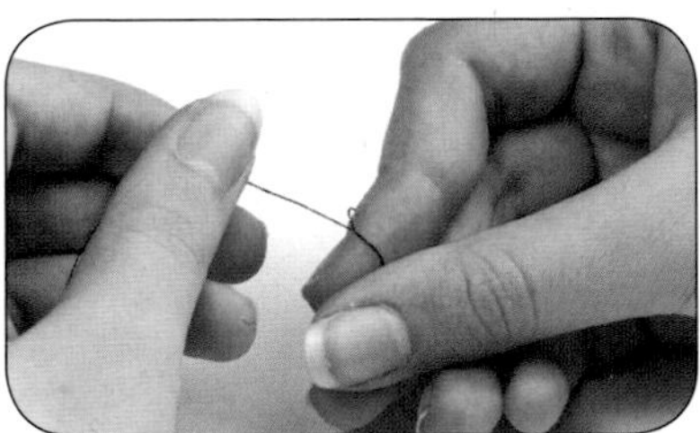

ABOVE Slide your forefinger back along your thumb.

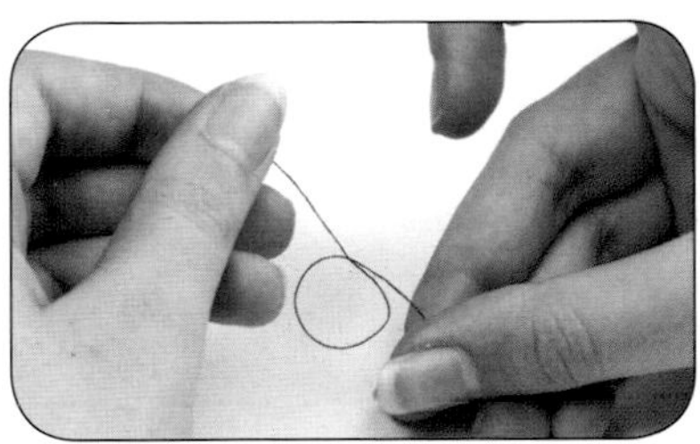

ABOVE Then pull at the knot to make it tighter.

Question 32:
How do I secure my stitches to begin?

To secure your thread when beginning to hand sew, make sure that the thread is knotted and that the knot is large enough to not pull through your fabric. (You'll need larger knots for looser fabrics.) You should always pull the needle through from the wrong side of the fabric (inside of the garment) to the right side. If this is not possible, and you are sewing on the outside of the garment, then try to hide the knot in a seam or pleat, or under a button. Then slide the needle and thread through a few strands of the fabric and begin mending or sewing.

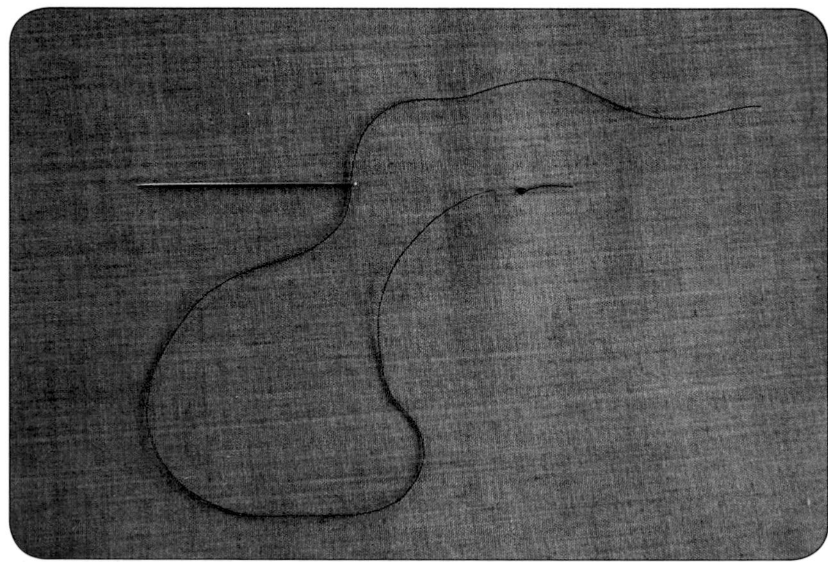

ABOVE After you've knotted the end of the thread, you should start your stitching on the wrong side of the fabric.

Question 33:
How do I end the stitching?

When you get to the end of the thread or are finished stitching, you need to knot the thread so the stitches do not start coming out. Stop stitching when the thread is still 10–12.5cm (4–5in) long. With the needle pulled to the wrong side of the fabric, take a tiny backstitch (see Question 43) and pull the thread through, leaving a small loop. Insert the needle and thread through the loop and pull to close the loop. Don't pull too tight; just enough so that the loop closes and lies flat on the fabric. According to the thickness of the thread and the fabric, one or two knots should be fine to avoid the knot slipping through the fabric and the threads coming out. But, if not, make a few more as necessary.

If you are working with double thread, you can knot the thread as explained above or by simply tying the two strands together. Pull the needle and thread through to the wrong side of the fabric; cut the needle off of the thread and cut the thread to 10–12.5cm (4–5in) long (or you can wait and cut the thread after knotting). Pull the two strands of thread apart and tie them together. Once again, you can make a few knots here if you feel that the thread may pull through the fabric. Trim off the loose end.

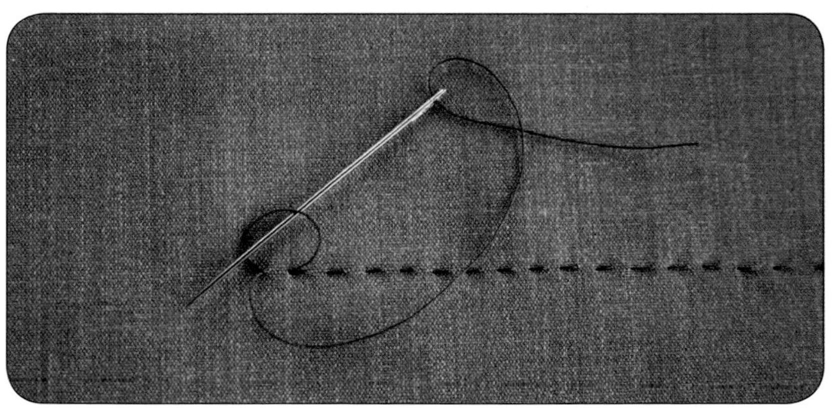

ABOVE When you get to the end of your stitching, take a small backstitch but don't pull the thread through fully. Insert the needle in the resulting loop to make a knot.

Question 34: What does 'rip-out' mean?

To 'rip-out' is a sewing term that means to take out the stitches. It's a strange term since it does not mean what it sounds like; you don't actually rip the stitches out. You may cut them – either with scissors or a seam ripper (see Question 35) – but then you need to tease out each stitch gently. If you pulled at a garment in an attempt to rip stitches out, you might actually tear the fabric and cause other threads to break.

Question 35: What is the best tool to use for ripping out?

Rather unsurprisingly, the best tool to use for ripping out is a seam ripper. This small and inexpensive tool is an essential part of your sewing kit. It has a pointed tip that you can insert between and under stitches you want to rip out, and a small curved blade that you use to actually cut the thread. It can also be used to cut very small areas of fabric, such as when making buttonholes. Take care when using a seam ripper, however; it's sharper than it looks!

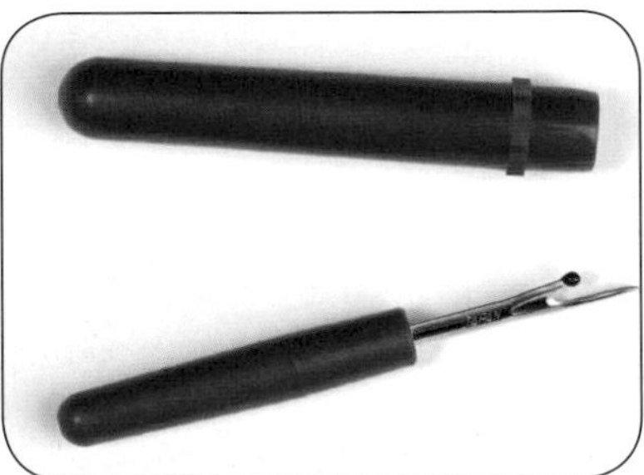

ABOVE A seam ripper usually comes with a lid that protects the pointed end.

Question 36:
What is an overlocker?

An overlocker (also known as a serger) is a special machine that trims and finishes off seam edges so that they do not fray. When you stitch a seam with an overlocker, it also encloses the seam allowance (or edge of the fabric) inside a thread casing, and trims off excess fabric – all in one step.

Overlockers used to be used only in the textile and fashion industry, however in the past 20 years or so, they have become increasingly popular in home sewing. While using an overlocker will not be discussed in this book, it is mentioned in Chapter 5, when describing the different types of seam closures and finishes. If, however, you want to take sewing further and plan to do some dressmaking, then you may well want to consider using one.

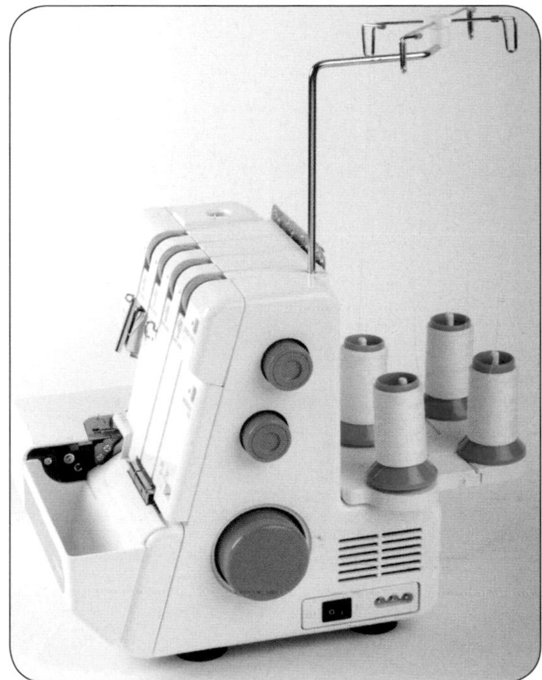

LEFT A overlocker does not look like a conventional sewing machine and yet it can do many of the same tasks.

Question 37:
What is topstitching?

Topstitching is a type of stitching, often a little longer than normal stitching, that is done on the right side of the fabric through all layers. Topstitching is usually used for decoration and to hold several layers of fabrics together. It is used most often on garment edges, such as necklines and hems, where it helps facings to stay in place. It gives a crisp edge. Topstitching designed to be decorative can be done in a different colour thread than the garment. Otherwise, topstitching is done with thread that matches the garment colour.

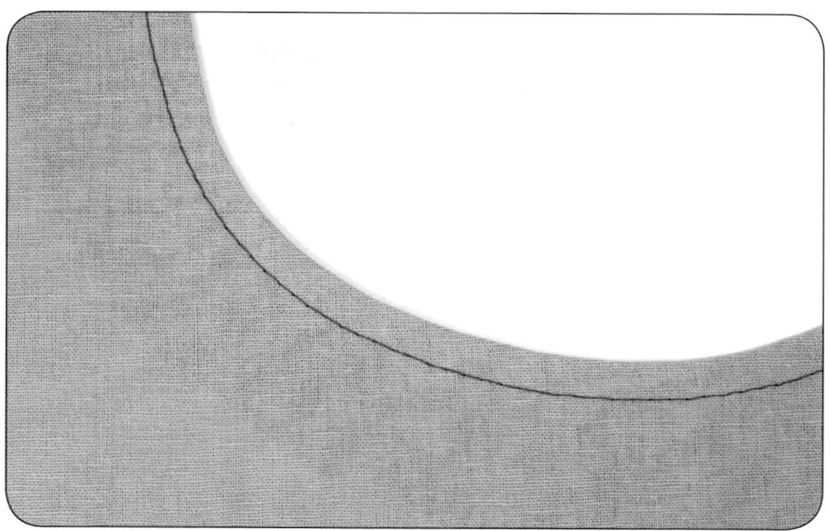

ABOVE A line of topstitching around a neckline gives a garment a neat finish. Using a different coloured thread to the fabric adds an element of decoration.

Question 38:
What are the basic sewing stitches that would be most useful?

With any new skill, you'll soon discover that there are many different ways to get to the end results. This is as true in sewing and in hand mending, you'll find there are numerous types of stitches that can be used.

Over the next few pages, you will find descriptions of some of the most useful basic stitches, plus information on how to do them. These stitches will be referenced in the following chapters in explaining how to fix and alter certain items.

The stitches are: tacking stitch, hemming stitch, catch stitch, slip stitch, backstitch, and overcast or blanket stitch.

Tacking stitch allows you to hold pieces together temporarily while you do hand or machine mending. It can also be used to mark fabric; for example, the position of a button.

Hemming and catch stitches are used when you repair an existing hem or turn up a new one. They are preferable to machine sewing because they barely show on the right side of a garment.

Slip stitch and backstitch are ideal when you want to mend a seam. And blanket stitch (also known as overcast stitch) is a great stitch to use if you want to finish hems or sew on patches with a decorative stitch.

Once you have mastered these basic stitches, you can decide for yourself which may be easiest or more appropriate for your own mending jobs.

Question 39:
What is tacking stitch and how do I do it?

Tacking stitches are extra-long stitches used to keep layers of fabric together while you do the regular stitching – by hand or machine. Basting is usually done by hand with a contrasting colour thread, so it can be seen easily and then removed.

To tack, begin by threading the needle and knot the thread for a single thread (see Question 31). It does not matter on which side you begin (right or wrong side) because the tacking stitches will most likely be taken out afterward. (There are rare instances when tacking stitches remain in the garment after completion for more stability). Take several large and evenly spaced stitches with the needle and then pull the needle and thread up. Keep going until you have finished tacking the two pieces together. Then pull the needle off the thread. Again, these are temporary stitches and will be taken out so you really do not need to knot the thread when you finish stitching.

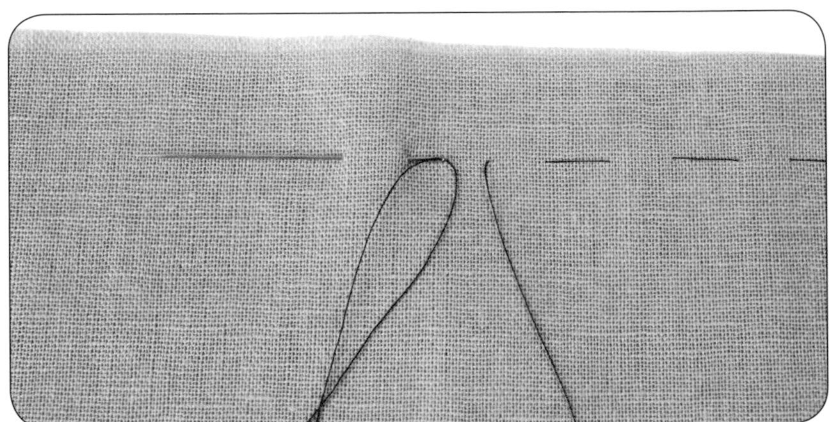

ABOVE Make long even stitches when tacking; they'll hold the fabric layers together more effectively than uneven, messy stitches.

Question 40:
What is hemming stitch and how do I do it?

Hemming stitch is a slanted stitch that's worked by hand along a turned hem to secure it. You take large stitches in the turned hem and small stitches in the single layer of fabric; these show on the right side so need to be very small.

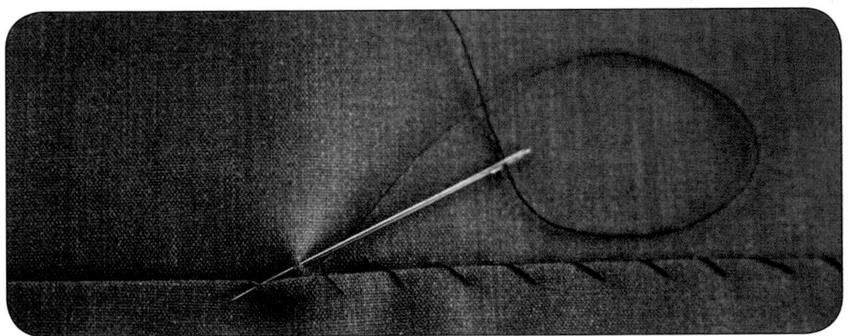

HOW IT'S DONE

- Start by knotting the thread and then secure it inside the hem. Pull the needle and thread through the fold of the hem, close to the folded edge.
- Pick up a few threads from the fabric above the hem, about 1cm (3⁄8in) from where the needle came out.
- Insert the needle through the folded hem edge at the same time.
- Draw the thread through, then continue making stitches in the same way.
- Work your way along the hem, making the stitches as invisible as possible on the right side.
- Practise to get a good, even stitch and the look you want on the outside of your garment.
- Don't pull the thread too tight as you work, or the stitches are more likely to show on the right side.
- Knot the thread close to the fabric and cut off the remaining thread.

Question 41:
What is catch stitch and how do I do it?

Catch stitch is another type of hemming stitch. In this variation small stitches are taken in both the folded hem edge and in the fabric above the hem. On the wrong side, it looks like the embroidery stitch called herringbone stitch.

This stitch is worked from left to right. If you are left handed, reverse the instructions given here.

HOW IT'S DONE

- Secure your thread and bring the needle through the hem as for hemming stitch (see Question 40).
- Take a very small stitch in the fabric above the hem, just a little way to the right, inserting the needle from right to left.
- Take the next stitch in the hem, just a little way to the right, again inserting the needle from right to left.
- Continue along the hem. Finish as for hemming stitch.

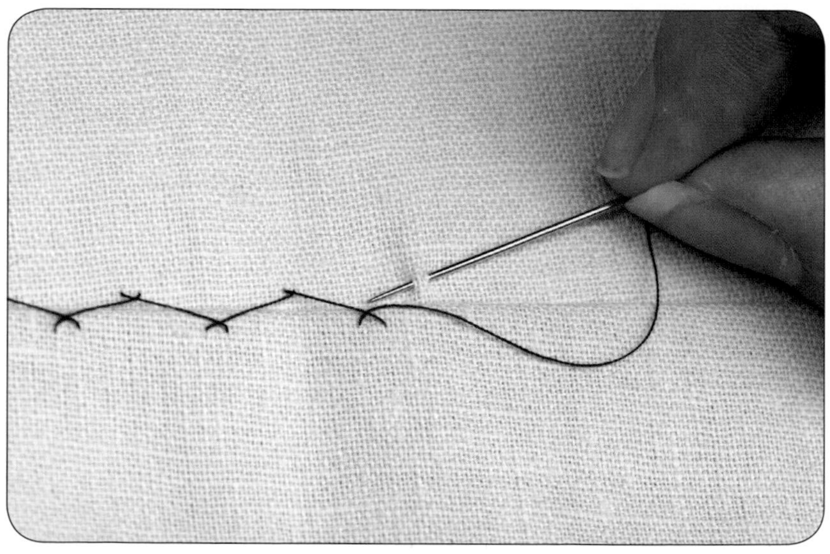

Question 42:
What is slip stitch and how do I do it?

Slip stitch is a very useful stitch. It's used to join two folded edges of fabric, making it ideal for mending seams, especially when the seam allowances are sewn down and you can't restitch along the original. You can hold your sewing so that you work from right to left, or from bottom to top, whichever is easier for you.

HOW IT'S DONE

- Thread your needle with a single thread and knot it.
- Bring the needle out through one edge, and make a small stitch in the fold of the opposite edge.
- Draw the thread through, then take another small stitch in the opposite edge.
- Continue stitching, alternating between the edges.

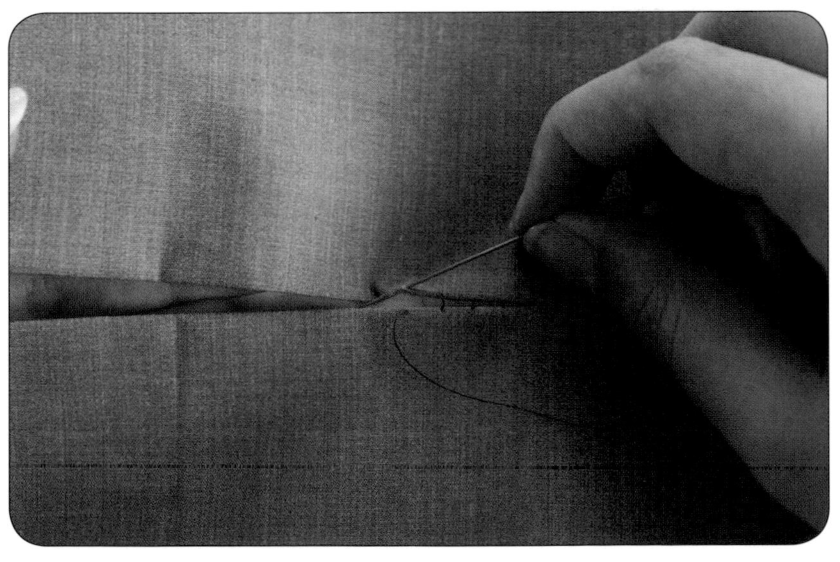

Question 43:
What is backstitch and how do I do it?

The backstitch is one of the strongest and most versatile hand-mending stitches. You double back over the stitches as you work, so reinforcing the line of stitching. This makes it ideal for mending seams or other areas that need a secure stitch. Full backstitch, when done neatly, can look similar to sewing-machine stitching.

To get started, use a single thread, thread the needle and knot the thread. Bring the needle and thread through to the right side of the fabric. Then insert the needle in the fabric approximately 3mm (⅛in) behind the point where the needle and thread first came up. Pull the thread through. Then bring the needle and thread back out to the right side about 3mm (⅛in) in front of the stitch just made. To make the second stitch, insert the needle at the same point where the thread first came up. Continue making stitches in this way until the work is completed (see below).

You can also use a half backstitch; this is similar to the backstitch in the way it is worked except that you leave a stitch length between the stitches as you work. In other words, you make the stitch that you take backwards 3mm (⅛in) long, but then bring the needle back through to the right side 6mm (¼in) from the stitch.

HOW IT'S DONE

- Bring the needle and thread out at A.
- Insert the needle again at B.
- Then bring the needle out again a stitch-length ahead of A, at the point labelled C.
- Insert the needle again at A.

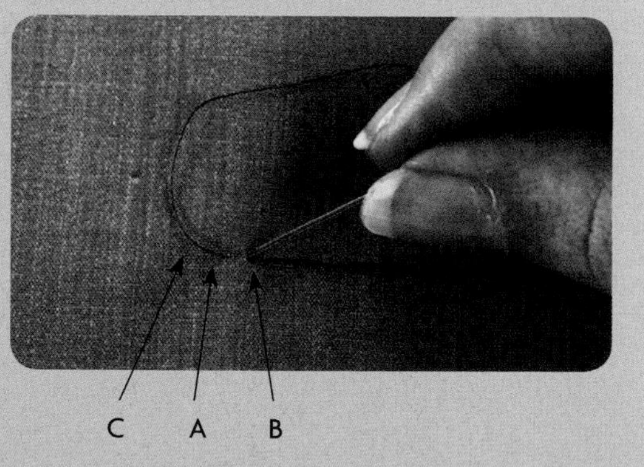

Question 44:
What is overcast or blanket stitch and how do I do it?

Blanket stitch is used as a decorative way to finish the edges of fabric. It can be used to finish turned hems – as is seen on old-fashioned wool blankets – or to finish the raw edges of any fabric than doesn't fray, such as felt or modern fleece. It can also be used to fix patches in place (see Question 79) or to add an appliquéd decoration, or as a stitch for mending frayed buttonholes.

You can use ordinary sewing thread, but embroidery floss or doubled thread is more effective and looks more decorative.

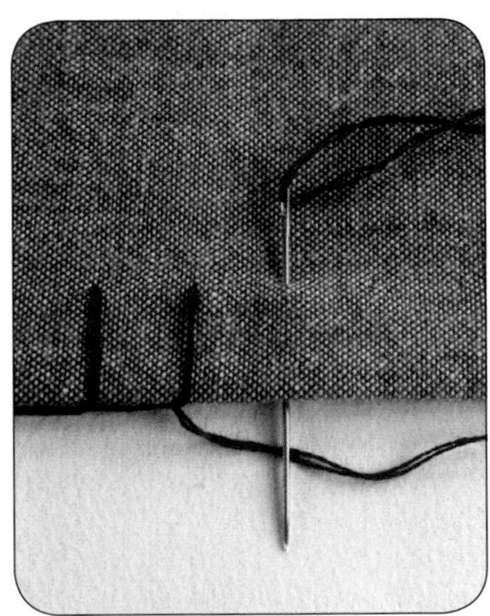

HOW IT'S DONE

- First thread your needle and secure the thread on the underside of the work. Use several strands of embroidery floss if you want to create a thick, decorative stitch.
- Bring the needle and thread through to the right side of the fabric below the outside edge.
- Insert the needle through the right side of the fabric, where you want the first stitch to begin.
- Push it through all the layers of fabric and down towards the edge.
- Keeping the thread under the point of the needle, draw the needle and thread through to form a stitch.
- Continue in the same way keeping the depth of the stitches and the distance between them even.

45 What types of buttons are available?

46 How do I sew on a two-holed button?

47 How do I sew on a four-holed button?

48 What is a button shank?

49 When would you use a shank button rather than a sew-through button?

50 How do you sew on buttons with a shank?

51 How can I fix fraying buttonholes?

52 The bottom button on my long coat keeps pulling off; how can I fix this?

53 What are the two parts of a press stud?

54 Where can press studs be used?

55 How are press studs sewn on?

56 Why doesn't my garment hang flat after I have sewn on new buttons or press studs?

57 What are hooks and eyes?

58 What are the different types of hooks and eyes?

59 How do you sew on a hook?

60 How do I sew on the eye or bar?

61 How do I make a loop for a hook out of thread?

62 The hooks in the waistband of ready-made trousers keep popping out; can I fix this?

63 What are the parts of a zip?

64 What types of zip are there?

65 Is it worth fixing a zip?

66 How do I know what's wrong with my zip?

67 How can I stop the teeth catching as I open or close the zip?

68 How do I fix a zip that is tearing away from the fabric?

69 How do I fix a zip that is stuck?

70 How do I fix a zip when the zip pull has fallen off?

3
BUTTONS, ZIPS AND OTHER CLOSURES

Question 45:
What types of buttons are available?

There are two different types of buttons – sew-through buttons and shank buttons. The different names are based on how they are attached to fabric.

Sew-through buttons are pierced with either two or four holes. The needle and thread goes through the holes and into the fabric several times to attach this type of button to the fabric.

Shank buttons have a loop on the back which is either made of metal or of the same material of the button. The shank can be quite small and close to the button, or quite prominent. Stitches are made through this loop to attach the button to the fabric.

Sew-through and shank buttons come in many, many different materials, shapes, sizes and colours. Buttons may also be covered to coordinate with a garment.

EXPERT TIP

“Buttons are a great way to bring out your creativity. There are so many different styles of buttons – all shapes, sizes and designs, some cheap, some expensive. You can use them to spruce up a jacket or coat, or even to create a decorative trim (see Question 191). You can add even more decorative detail by stitching sew-through buttons on with a contrasting thread.”

ABOVE When you've been sewing for a while, you'll build up your own collection of useful different buttons.

Question 46:
How do I sew on a two-holed button?

Mark the place where the button is to go with tailor's chalk, a disappearing marking pen or crossed pins. If you are replacing a button that has fallen off, keep the old thread in place for placement of the new button.

Thread a needle with double thread and knot the ends together. Push the needle through the fabric from the wrong to right side. Pull the needle and thread up and insert in the first hole of the button. Pull the thread all the way up and then insert in the second hole of the button and back into the fabric. Pull the thread through to the wrong side, then push up through the fabric again into the first hole. Pull the thread all the way up before inserting in the second hole again. Do this a few times, keeping the thread taut, but not too tight. Bring the thread to the wrong side of the fabric; knot and cut the thread.

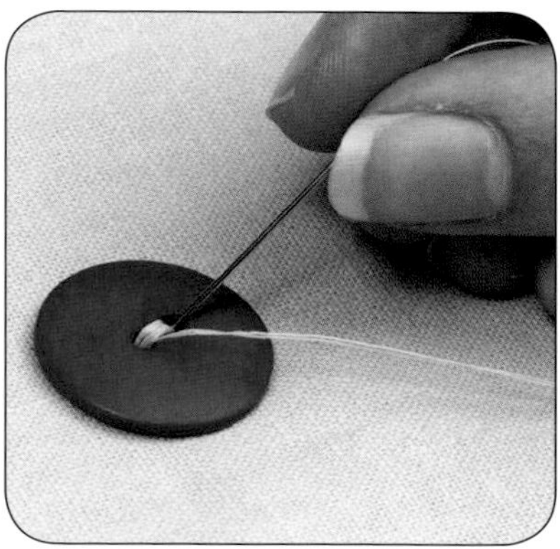

ABOVE Take several stitches through the holes of the button and into the fabric to adequately secure it in place.

EXPERT TIP

“Buttons should never be sewn on very tight. If they are too tight, the fabric will pucker and possibly begin to rip when the buttons are buttoned. To make sure that a sew-through button is not sewn on too tight, a simple trick can be used. Mark the exact spot where the button is to be sewn with a pin or pins. Keep the pins in the fabric until the button is completely sewn on. The little bit of space that the pins take up will stop the thread from being pulled too tight. Alternatively, slide a toothpick or a spent match under the button after the first stitch has been made.”

Question 47:
How do I sew on a four-holed button?

As when sewing on a two-holed button, use double thread and knot the thread. Mark the exact place where the button should be sewn.

First sew on the button through two holes only, as described in Question 46. You can sew through two holes next to each other or diagonally opposite. Then bring the thread back to the wrong side of the fabric and up through one of the unstitched holes. Insert the needle in the remaining hole and back through to the wrong side of the fabric. After you have gone through these holes a few times, knot the thread on the wrong side of the fabric and cut. Four-holed buttons can be sewn with parallel lines or criss-crossed lines.

EXPERT TIP

“It is best not to go from hole one to hole two and then to holes three and four and back to holes one and two. This will only leave an awful mess on the wrong side of your fabric. Sew the first pair of holes, with several stitches, before moving on to the next holes.”

ABOVE If you stitch through holes that are diagonally opposite each other, you will leave a criss-cross pattern of thread on a four-holed button.

Question 48:
What is a button shank?

A button shank is the loop on the back of some buttons. Shanks provide a small amount of space for the fabric to sit in between the button and the garment when the garment is buttoned. Unlike an ordinary sew-through button, a button with a shank has no holes in the top. The shank can be integral to the button; in other words, made of the same material as the button. It can also be made of a different material, usually metal, that's attached to the back of the button.

ABOVE Shank buttons come in all shapes and sizes. The shank is the small loop on the back of the button, through which these buttons are sewn to the fabric.

Question 49: When would you use a shank button rather than a sew-through button?

The main reason why you would use a shank button over a two- or four-holed button is that sometimes you need a button that protrudes a little. This is particularly the case in any garment made with a thicker fabric such as tweed or gabardine. If the fabric is thick, you want the button to stick out a little if it is to lie flat on the outside of the garment when done up.

Most heavier, cold-weather coats and jackets use shank buttons. However, you can use a shank button almost anywhere.

LEFT Shank buttons are ideal for jackets or coats made of thicker fabrics.

Question 50:
How do you sew on buttons with a shank?

Mark the exact spot where the button should be sewn. Thread a needle with double thread and knot the ends together. Push the needle through the fabric from the wrong to right side. Holding the button with one hand, insert the needle in the button shank and then back into the fabric, close to where the needle came out. Pull the thread all the way through to the wrong side of the fabric. Then push the needle back through to the right side of the fabric, emerging close to where the button sits. Pull the thread all the way through and then insert the needle in the shank. Take the needle back into the fabric again. Do this three to four times, until the button is secure.

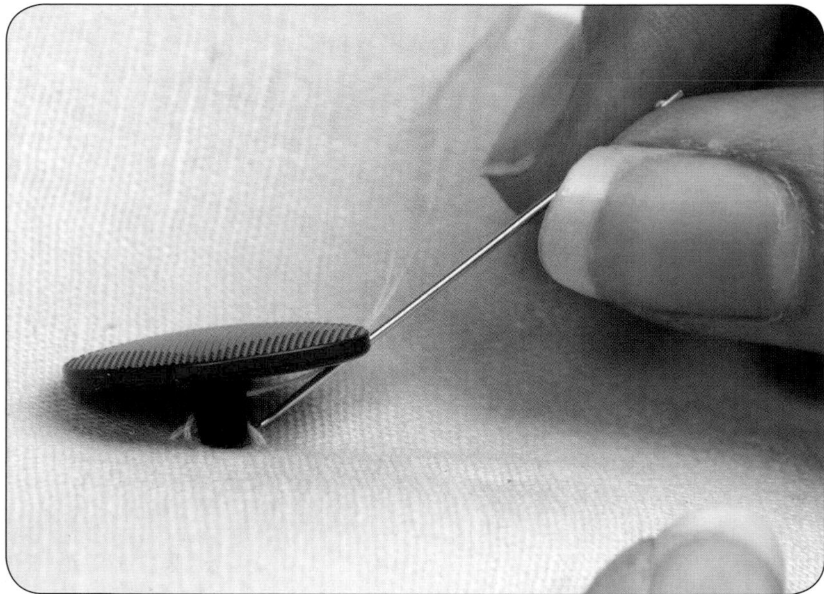

ABOVE The more stitches you make, the tighter the button will sit on the fabric; you may have to angle the needle to insert it near the button shank.

Question 51:
How can I fix fraying buttonholes?

Fraying buttonhole threads not only make a garment look untidy but they also may lead to your buttons popping open with just the slightest pull. You do not need a sewing machine with a buttonhole feature to fix this problem. First, if the threads of the buttonhole are just fraying in a very small area, you can try using Fray Check (or in an emergency, some clear nail varnish). This may stiffen the fabric a little, but should be fine. Always test the Fray Check or clear nail varnish on a seam allowance to make sure that it does not discolour the fabric.

If a large part of the buttonhole is frayed, you can use blanket stitch (see Question 44) to mend the buttonhole. With small scissors, carefully cut off the threads that are broken and fraying (you can leave the threads that still remain in place). Choose a thread that matches as closely as possible to the buttonhole thread already used; a contrasting colour has been used in the illustration here to make the stitching clearer. Using double thread, work blanket stitch around the frayed area, making the stitches small and very close together.

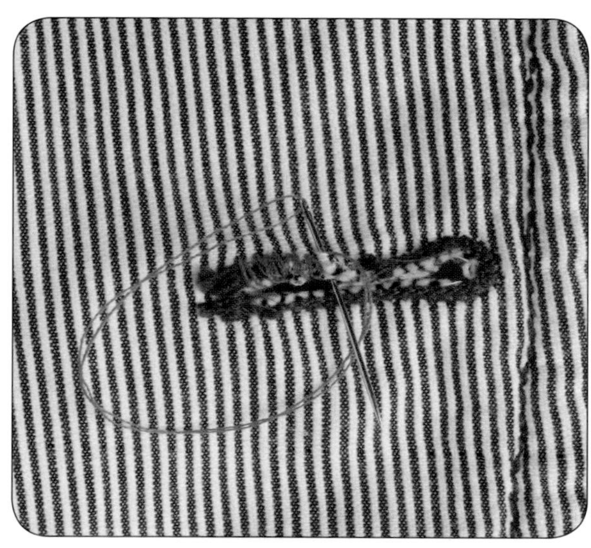

LEFT To repair the edge of a buttonhole where the stitching has frayed, work blanket stitches very close together around the area to be mended.

Question 52:
The bottom button on my long coat keeps pulling off; how can I fix this?

The last button on a coat – the one at the bottom – can be put under a lot of stress. As you walk along, it is the button that is most likely to be pulled open by the motion of your legs. And when you sit down with the coat buttoned up, this part of the coat spreads apart and the button can pop open. If this happens continually, the button may start to pull off and need sewing back on regularly. The fabric may even start to rip at the position of the button.

If this becomes a problem with your coat, there is a simple solution; take the button off and then sew it back on again with elastic thread. You will probably have to use a thicker needle than usual, with a thicker eye to accommodate the elastic thread. The elastic will stretch when you sit down and reduce the stress on the button.

Elastic thread usually only comes in black or white. Choose the colour that is best for your coat. If the button is a shank button, then the thread colour will not matter so much, especially on the last button. However, if the button is two- or four-holed, there is something you can do to make the stitching match. After sewing the button on, take a piece of thread the same colour as the thread used for the other buttons and sew over the elastic thread. Sew through the holes without catching the fabric. Do this three to four times and the elastic thread on top of the button will be hidden by the stitching.

Question 53:
What are the two parts of a press stud?

The two parts of a press stud fastening are usually called the ball and socket parts. The ball part is the flatter part with the protruding piece that fits into the socket half. The socket part is more rounded and has the space for the ball part to go into.

Press studs are often used on infant and baby clothes for a few reasons; they are easier for children to use, plus they are attached flat against the fabric making it harder for younger children to put them in their mouths and possibly separate them from the fabric and swallow.

ABOVE Press studs are generally made from plastic or metal. The metal ones can be either metallic and silvery in colour, as here, or black or white.

Question 54:
Where can press studs be used?

Press studs can be used in almost any instance where you don't want the closure to be visible. They are used on openings where one piece of a garment overlaps another and the overlap is made up of two or more layers of fabric, such as at a waistband or cuff. The ball part of the press stud is usually stitched to the underside of the overlap and, if the stitching is done with care, there should be nothing showing on the right, outer side of the garment.

They are very useful to correct any gaping in an item of clothing. If you have a cross-over top that doesn't lay well over the bust, or that keeps falling open, then a press stud stitched at the point where the top gapes will fix the problem. You can also use press studs on shirts and blouses to eliminate any embarrassing gaps that might occur between the buttons.

ABOVE Plastic press studs are ideal for securing lighter weight fabrics.

Question 55:
How are press studs sewn on?

Start by marking the exact placement for the press stud. If you are replacing a press stud and there are still threads from the old one remaining, leave these to mark where the new one will be sewn. Thread the needle with a double thread and secure on the wrong side of the fabric. Bring the needle up to the right side at the point where the ball part of the press stud is to be placed, and then insert it through one of the holes on the press stud, from the underside. Insert the needle in the fabric, close to where the needle and thread came up, and pull the thread through to make the first stitch. Make four or five more stitches through the first hole of the press stud, before moving on to the next hole. Try not to make the stitches radiate out too far into the fabric, and don't do too many, or the result will be too bulky. When all four holes are stitched through, secure the thread on the wrong side and snip it off. Then mark the position of the socket part (see Expert Tip below) and stitch in place the same way, making sure that your stitches are not visible on the right side of your fabric.

ABOVE When sewing on either part of the press stud, stitch through one hole first, before moving on to the next.

EXPERT TIP

“After the ball part of the press stud is stitched in place, rub some tailor's chalk on to the ball and then overlap the edges of the garment as they will be when the opening is closed. Press down on the ball part to transfer the chalk to the fabric and perfectly mark the position of the socket part.”

Question 56:
Why doesn't my garment hang flat after I have sewn on new buttons or press studs?

If a garment is not hanging flat, the most likely cause is that the button or press stud has not been sewn in the exact correct place. It is very important to mark the exact placement of the button or press stud before you begin. To fix the problem, unfasten the garment and lay it flat or hang it up. Place a mark (tailor's chalk, disappearing pen or pins in a cross formation) where the button or snap should be. Is it where you had just sewn it? Even the tiniest of changes will make a difference in how a garment hangs. For buttons, mark or place a pin right through the buttonhole.

LEFT Make a mark on your garment where the button should be – use pins or a marker – and then unpick the button and move to the right position.

Question 57:
What are hooks and eyes?

Hook-and-eye closures (often simply known as 'hooks') are a type of clothing fastener that consists of two parts; the first part is sewn to one of the pieces of fabric that need to be fastened, the second part is stitched to the other piece of fabric. One part of the closure is a small hook; the other part is a small loop, which is also known as the 'eye'. To fasten the garment, the hook is slotted into the loop. Hooks and eyes are sewn on in a similar way to press studs, with the thread going in and out of the holes at the bottom of the hook, and in the eye.

BELOW Both hooks and eyes are made out of metal wire. This is bent into loops at the bottom of each hook and eye; the hook or eye is stitched in place through these loops.

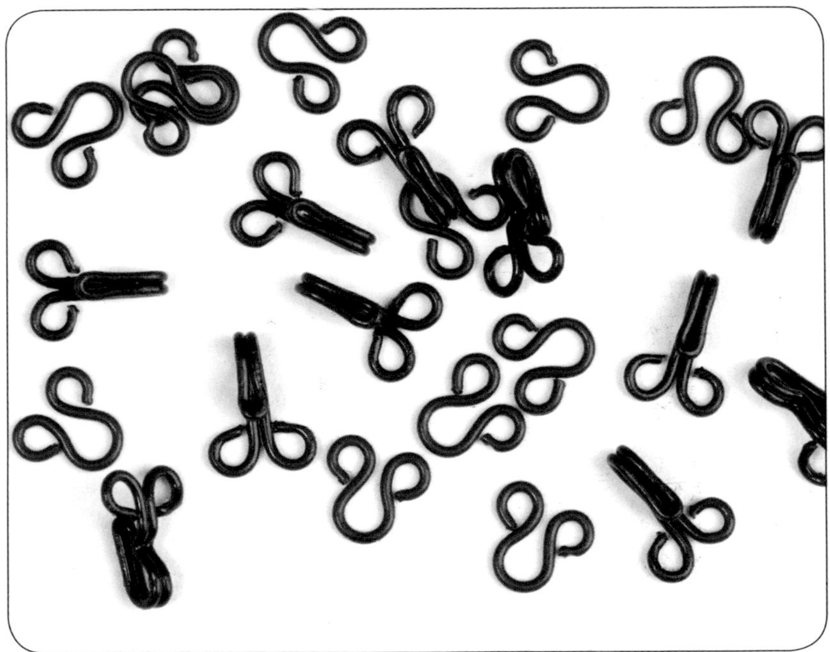

Question 58:
What are the different types of hooks and eyes?

There are several types of hooks and eyes. One type of hook is that which is sewn above a zipper in a women's dress, top or skirt. Another type is that used for the waistbands of trousers. This type is a little different from a regular hook and eye. The hook is wider and flatter and the eye is shaped like a bar. There are also several types of eyes – a straight eye, bar eye, round eye and thread chain eye.

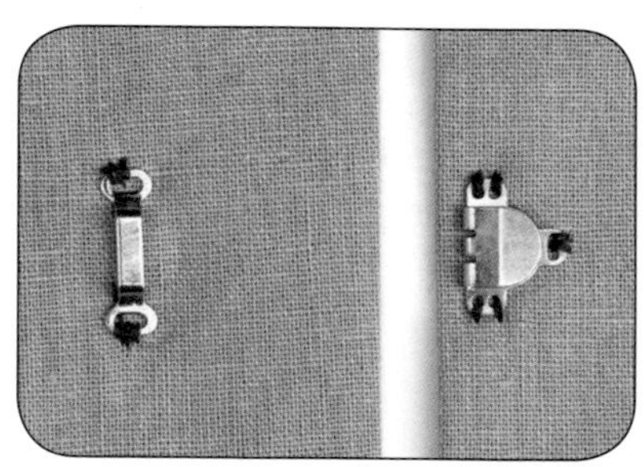

ABOVE The flat style of the hook-and-bar-eye type closure is ideal for openings that you want to lie flat, such as the waistbands of trousers.

Question 59:
How do you sew on a hook?

A hook and eye is sewn on very similarly to a press stud – pulling the threads up through the fabric and then down into one of the holes of the hook.

The hook is usually sewn on first. Mark the spot where it will be sewn on by holding the two pieces of cloth or edges together and make a mark where you want it to be. On an overlapping edge, position the hook on the underside of the overlap, face up and about 5mm (¼in) in from the fabric edge so it cannot be seen from the outside. On an opening where the edges butt up against each other – at the waistband of a skirt with a grown-on waistband, for example – position the hook so that the end falls close to, but not touching, the edge.

To sew on hooks, begin by holding the hook in place with your thumb and let the edge of the hook

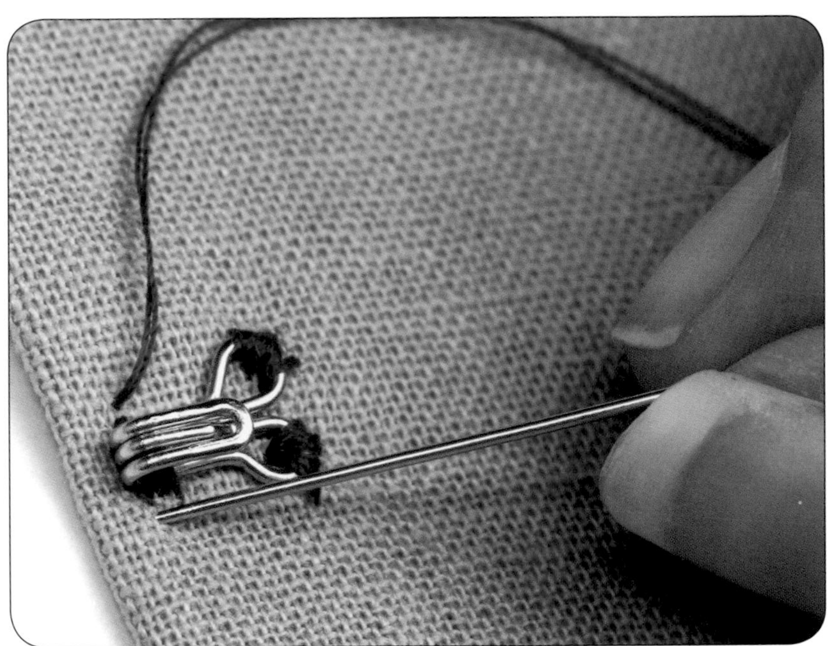

ABOVE Once you have stitched through the holes at the bottom of a hook, take a few stitches across the hook itself to hold it down.

come where your mark is. Insert the needle in the wrong side of the fabric and bring up to the right side next to one of the holes at the base of the hook. Pull the thread all the way through. (Regular hooks usually have two holes to sew down and waistband hooks usually have three holes to sew down. If sewing on the type with three holes, sew through the middle hole first to stop the hook from sliding around when the other holes are sewn down.)

Push the needle into the hole, into the fabric and down on to the wrong side. Pull the thread all the way through. Then push the needle back through to the right side, as close to where the first stitch began as possible. Then insert the needle back in the hole of the hook and draw through to the wrong side. Do this three to four times and then move on to the next hole. When you have completed sewing through all the holes, bring the needle back up to the right side next to the hook part of the hook. Make a few stitches across the hook to secure it firmly, so it doesn't pull away from the fabric. Take the needle to the wrong side and finish off securely.

Question 60:
How do I sew on the eye or bar?

The eye or bar part of a hook-and-eye closure is sewn in place after the hook has been secured. To get the position of the eye or bar on an overlapping edge, bring the edges of the opening together and mark where the end of the hook falls on the underlap; this is where you need to stitch the eye or bar. On an opening where the edges butt up against each other the eye is positioned opposite the hook and extending slightly beyond the edge.

To stitch either an eye or bar in place, bring your needle and thread through to the right side of the fabric at the position that you've marked. Hold the eye or bar in place with a finger or thumb and then push the needle through one of the holes and into the fabric. Take several stitches through the same hole until it's secure. Then pass the needle through the fabric to the position of the next hole: if you're stitching to more than one layer of fabric, you can conceal this within the fabric; if you're stitching to a single layer, take a few small stitches across to the next hole. Bring the needle to the right side and then insert in the hole and into the fabric. Take several stitches through the same hole. When all holes in the eye are secured, take the needle through to the wrong side and fasten off securely.

Question 61:
How do I make loop for a hook out of thread?

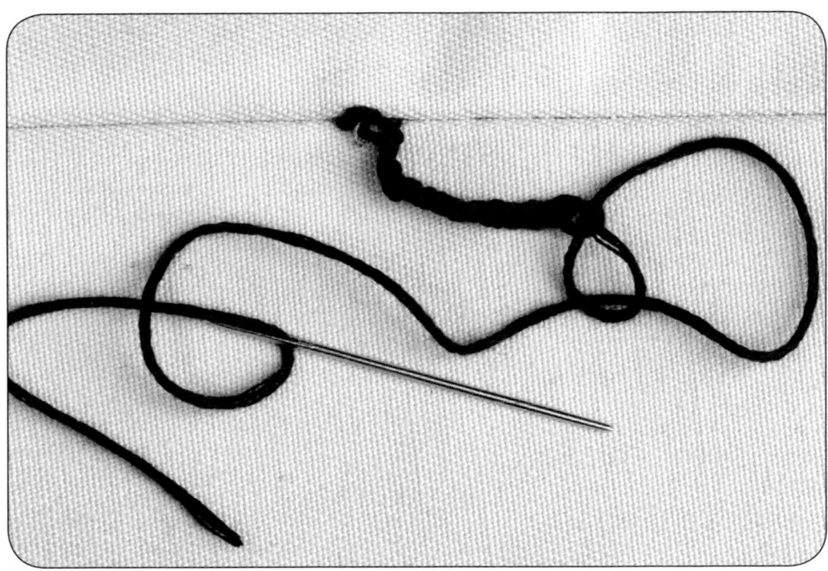

ABOVE You can use a length of thread, looped into chains, to create an 'eye' for a hook. Use embroidery thread to get a thick finished chain.

Secure the thread on the wrong side of the fabric and then bring to the right side. Insert the needle in the fabric close to the place where the thread emerges and push the needle through. Draw the thread through but not completely; leave a small loop on the right side. Bring the needle out again on the right side. Hold the loop open with the fingers on one hand, then use the other hand to pass the working thread (that still has the needle on it) through the loop. Pull a loop of the working thread through the first loop, then pull on this to tighten the first loop. Repeat until you have reached the desired length; with the last loop, pull the working thread all the way through, and use the needle to secure the free end to your garment.

Question 62:
The hooks in the waistband of ready-made trousers keep popping out; can I fix this?

There are types of hooks and eyes used by the fashion industry that aren't sewn in; they take less labour time to assemble. They are attached by using prongs that clasp into the fabric. You usually see those on the waistbands of trousers. With just a little stress on the waistband, they have a habit of pulling out completely.

The easy way to fix this is to purchase a new sew-in type of hook and eye to replace the pronged hook and eye. Once the prong-hook pulls out, no matter how well you re-attach it to the fabric, it will most likely pull out again. Hooks are very inexpensive and are found in all sewing stores. Bar hooks are a little more difficult to find, but are usually found in major sewing stores.

EXPERT TIP

“ Since the clasp-type of hook and eye will pull out eventually, why not be proactive? Buy a few packets of hooks and eyes – most sewing stores should have at least one size, if not several – in a range of colours, and when you buy a new pair of trousers, replace clasp-type hooks and eyes with the sew-in sort you've bought. It is the bar half which normally pulls out first, so if you wish, just replace the bar. Do it right away, so the trousers do not end up in the mending pile! ”

Question 63:
What are the parts of a zip?

Before you can figure out if a zip can be fixed or needs replacing, or whether you can attempt the repair yourself or should hand it over to a tailor, you should know what the various parts of a zip are and how it is constructed.

A zip consists of two strips of fabric tape joined by shaped metal or plastic teeth. The slider is moved along the rows of teeth by the zip pull. Inside the slider is a Y-shaped channel that meshes together or separates the rows of teeth, depending on whether you are pulling the slider up or down. A metal stopper prevents the slider from coming off the end of the zip.

Problems often occur when the zip slider becomes worn and does not properly align and join (or part) the alternating teeth. If a zip fails, it can either get stuck or can partially break.

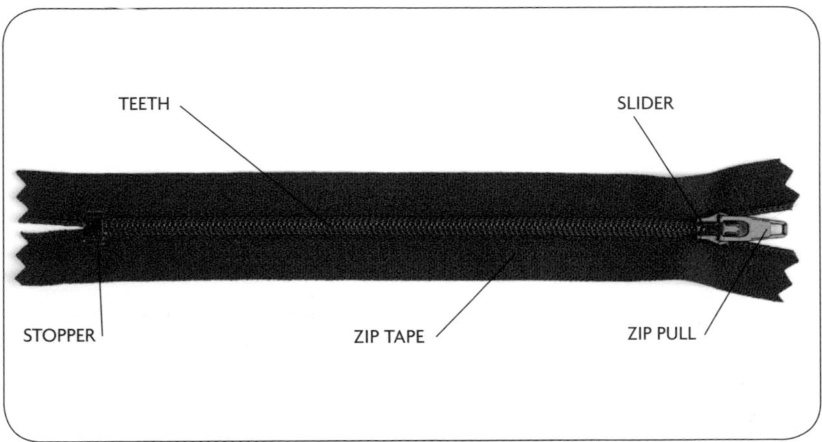

ABOVE A zip is made up of two lengths of tape with teeth along the edge of each. The teeth interlock when the zip pull draws the slider along the teeth.

Question 64:
What types of zip are there?

Coil zips are the most popular type of zip. The slider runs along two coils of teeth attached to lengths of tape on each side.

Invisible zips are, generally speaking, coil-type zips, with the teeth set on the underside of the tape to make them less prominent. The teeth and slider are the same colour as the zip tape and then this colour is matched to the garment. Invisible zips are commonly used in skirts and dresses.

Jeans, and other heavy-duty garments, use a metallic zip. The teeth are not set in a coil formation, but are made up of individual, moulded metal teeth which are positioned along the zip tape at regular intervals.

Open-ended zips are most often used in jackets and coats. They are particularly popular in all-weather type jackets, where you might want to open the bottom of the zip to make sitting down easier while still wearing the garment. Open-ended zips can be any of the above specified types. Closed-ended zips are closed at both ends; they are often used in bags and luggage.

Question 65:
Is it worth fixing a zip?

It's always worth mending a zip; why discard a garment if all that needs fixing is this simple closure? Replacing a zip in a ready-made garment is certainly something that can be done, but it is difficult and for the purposes of this book, I would recommend that you take any garment that needs a new zip to a tailor. However, there are zip problems that you can fix so you need to ascertain what is wrong with the zip and decide if it needs to be fixed or replaced.

Question 66:
How do I know what's wrong with my zip?

Zips are usually very sturdy closures, however sometimes things can go wrong. Years ago, all zips were made of metal only and were more sturdy as a result, but nowadays, as the demand for cheaper ready-made clothes grows, cheaper closures are increasingly used, and plastic zippers are often favoured. Zips sewn into home products, such as cushions or in sofa seat cushions, rarely need to be fixed or replaced because they do not have the stress that a garment would.

So, what are the things that can go wrong with a zip? Firstly, you may find that the teeth catch against each other, making it hard to open or close the zip. You can try re-aligning the teeth to fix this problem – see Question 67.

Secondly, the stitching that holds the zip in place may have broken or pulled out. This is usually easily repaired using a basic mending stitch (see Question 68). If the stitching needs to be done by machine for whatever reason, this is the point where you should take the garment to a tailor.

Thirdly, the zip may be completely stuck; the slider won't budge when you try to pull it up or down. If it's stuck on the garment itself, it may be possible to extract the stuck fabric (see Question 69). And lastly, the zip pull might have come off; this is often easy to fix (see Question 70).

EXPERT TIP

"If your zip seems to stick constantly, and if it's hard to pull the slider up and down the zip, try this simple fix before trying to realign the teeth. Take an ordinary graphite pencil and rub it along the zip's teeth. More often than not, this simple trick will make it easier to move the teeth up and down."

Question 67:

How can I stop the teeth catching as I open or close the zip?

Zips are pretty sturdy closures, but sometimes with continuous stress, they do break or come apart. Is the zip not lining up, are the teeth out of alignment? Sometimes the teeth on a zip do not line up correctly, causing the zip to catch. This is fixable, but you need a few supplies, such as a pair of pliers. Remove the metal stopper at the bottom of the zipper with a the pliers. Pull hard! Don't worry, you will not be reusing this piece. Zip the zipper all the way down to the bottom, stopping just below the last of the teeth. Don't pull it off completely.

Using your fingers, rearrange and straighten the teeth of the zip so that one side isn't bunched up and both sides are even. Slowly zip up the zip halfway, checking to make sure that all the teeth are interlocking correctly.

Using a needle and double thread (or topstitching thread), sew a few stitches where the metal stopper was. The stopper is actually being replaced with this stitching. Sew around and around the bottom of the zip until you have about six to eight stitches in place. Tie off in a knot on the back side of the zip.

Pull the zip all the way to the top. It shouldn't catch anymore. If the zip gets misaligned again one day, just remove the stitching with a seam ripper and repeat this simple fix.

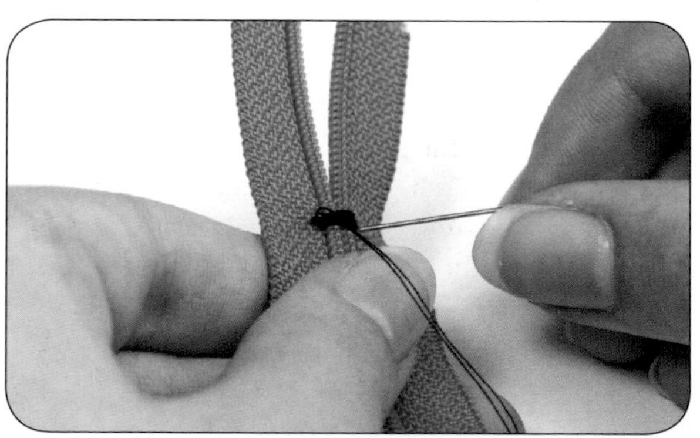

LEFT It's easy to remove the stopper on a zip and then finish the zip with stitching (the repair is shown here on an unattached zip for clarity's sake).

Question 68:
How do I fix a zip that is tearing away from the fabric?

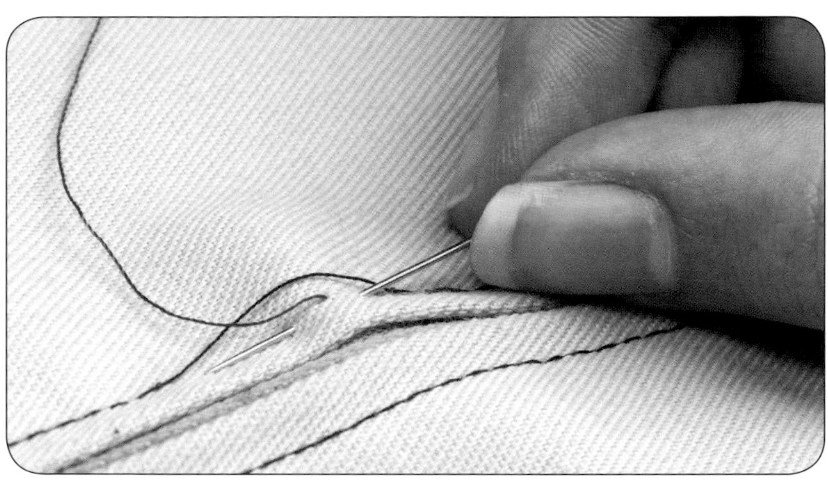

ABOVE To fix a zip sewn down with topstitching, work on the right side so you can make neat backstitches that follow the original machine stitching.

Generally speaking, zips are sewn into a seam by stitching them to the seam allowance. They can be sewn in so that there is topstitching on the right side of a garment, or to be invisible, and so are sewn to the allowance alone. Under stress, the zip can begin to tear away from the allowances. If the zip is still intact in the garment, then this is a very easy problem to fix.

Thread a needle with double thread and knot it. Turn the garment to the wrong side and secure the thread. Bring the needle to the right side and start to work backstitch (see Question 43), following the holes left by the ripped out stitches. When you get to the end, secure the thread on the wrong side; knot and cut off.

If you're repairing an invisible zip (one where there is no topstitching on the right side of the garment) you will work on the wrong side. Make sure that you stitch along the seam allowance and the zip tape, but not through to the right side.

Question 69:
How do I fix a zip that is stuck?

To fix a zip that is stuck, you must first find out what is stuck and why. Is the zip itself stuck because the plastic or metal is out of shape or is a piece of fabric stuck in the teeth of the zip?

Don't get frustrated and pull on the zip – that may break it. You can give it a gentle pull to see if it will go anywhere, then stop. Examine the zip to locate the problem. Is something caught in the teeth, such as the lining or a piece of thread from the seam allowance?

Very gently, try to pull the thread or lining away from the zip. Pull at the lining (which can be mended

EXPERT TIP

“ If you've got a zip that won't stay zipped, take small, needle-nose pliers and gently squeeze on the square bottom end of the zip pull, on both sides of the centre bar. ”

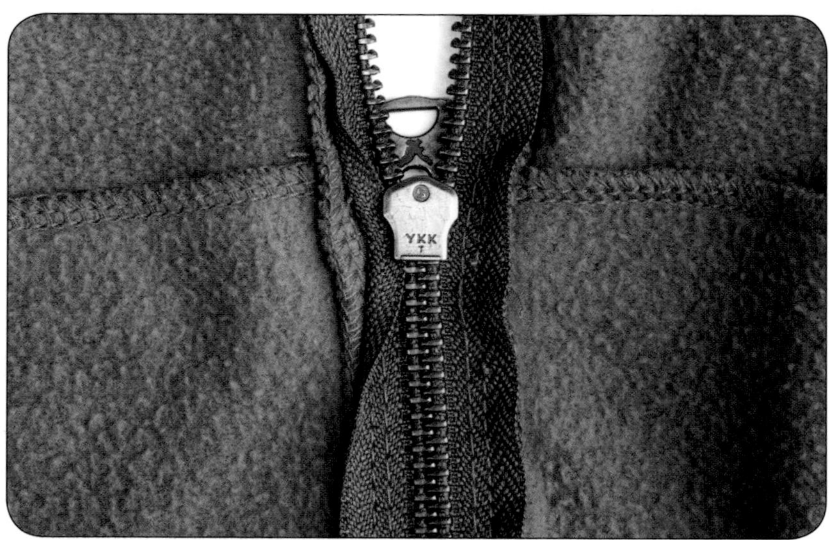

ABOVE If you've got the zip tape itself caught in the slider, take care when pulling it out to ensure that you don't damage the zip tape.

much more easily), not at the zip. Pulling the zip tab up or down will make the situation worse. If any of the teeth become separated as you pull out whatever is stuck, gently realign them.

If there is a lining, pull the lining away from the zip to prevent future snags. You may need to make a few stitches to tack the lining to the zip tape to keep it from catching in the zip again.

If the zip tape itself is caught in the slider, get hold of the tape either above or below the stuck area and pull it very gently away from the zip while you agitate the slider up and down very slightly. If it's hard to get hold of the zip tape, use a pair of tweezers.

When you've freed the slider, pull it to the bottom of the zip and then re-zip a few times, making sure that the lining or thread is out of the way and does not get caught.

Question 70:

How do I fix a zip when the zip pull has fallen off?

The pull that you use to move a zip slider up and down comes under a lot of stress. It's not surprising, therefore, that the metal loop that holds the pull on to the slider can sometimes open up and the pull can fall off.

Fortunately, this is probably the easiest zip repair of all. When the zip pull comes off, you simply buy another one to replace it. Zip pulls are sold in most sewing stores and in many other places too – look at online sewing suppliers for interesting selections. There are all different types of zip pulls – plain pulls, decorated pulls, children's pulls, and even designer pulls.

71 What supplies do I need to mend knitted items?

72 How can I fix the little snags on my sweaters or other knit garments?

73 How do I mend a hole in a knitted garment?

74 How do I darn?

75 What kind of holes are suitable for patching?

76 Where can I get patches?

77 Can I make my own patches?

78 How do I attach a patch to a garment?

79 How do I sew on a home-made patch or add decorative stitching?

80 What should I know about seams?

81 What are the different types of seam finishes?

82 How can I fix a ripped seam?

83 What are the methods to fix a tear in each seam closure?

84 My pockets always rip from keeping too much change in them; can they be fixed?

85 What types of hems are there and how wide should hems be?

86 How do I take the hem down on ready-made garments?

87 How do I prepare a skirt or trousers for hemming?

88 How do I turn up a hem in trousers, skirts or dresses?

89 What stitches do I use to hem?

90 What do I do if the hem circumference is very wide?

91 What do I do if the hem circumference is very narrow?

92 How do I hem the lining?

93 How do I mend a frayed hem?

94 Can I make the hem of my trousers longer at the back for when I wear heels?

95 How do I hem leather?

4

HAND MENDING KNOW-HOW

Question 71: What supplies do I need to mend knitted items?

To mend holes and snags in knitted garments, you can use sewing thread, yarn or embroidery thread that matches your knit garment in colour and weight. (Be aware that embroidery thread has a sheen to it and, therefore, it may stand out against the knit you are mending, even if you have matched the colour.) You will also need a needle with an eye large enough for the yarn or thread you have chosen to use. A small crochet hook may also come in handy to pull through snagged threads.

First, check the entire garment; is there just one small hole, a few snags or possibly moth holes throughout the garment? If you will be mending more than a small area (about 1cm (½in) square) and you still wish to keep the garment, you should try to purchase some yarn or wool that is as similar to the fibre the garment is made of as possible. If the sweater is wool and you cannot find wool yarn, that's fine, unless the hole you are patching is quite large (see Question 74).

For tiny holes and lightweight knits, you can use regular sewing thread or embroidery thread. The closer in colour and weight the thread or yarn is matched to the garment, the better your mending it will be hidden from sight.

ABOVE One of the great advantages of using embroidery thread to mend knits, is that it comes in a wide range of different colours.

Question 72:
How can I fix the little snags on my sweaters or other knit garments?

Fixing these snags and pulls is easy and will keep sweaters from looking old and washed out. Turn the sweater inside out. Insert a very small crochet hook from the wrong side through to the front at the site of the snag. Use the hook to pull the loose yarn through to the wrong side of the garment. According to how long the thread or yarn is that is pulled through, you can use the crochet hook to make a loop out of the loose yarn, then pull the loose end through the loop, creating a knot on the inside of the sweater. If the thread or yarn is long enough, make a knot and weave through a few strands of the sweater.

Alternatively, use a tiny bit of Fray Check or clear nail varnish on the end of the loose yarn – not the sweater itself. After the Fray Check (or clear nail varnish) has dried, turn the sweater right-side out and gently stretch it to smooth out any bunching in the fabric that the snag might have caused.

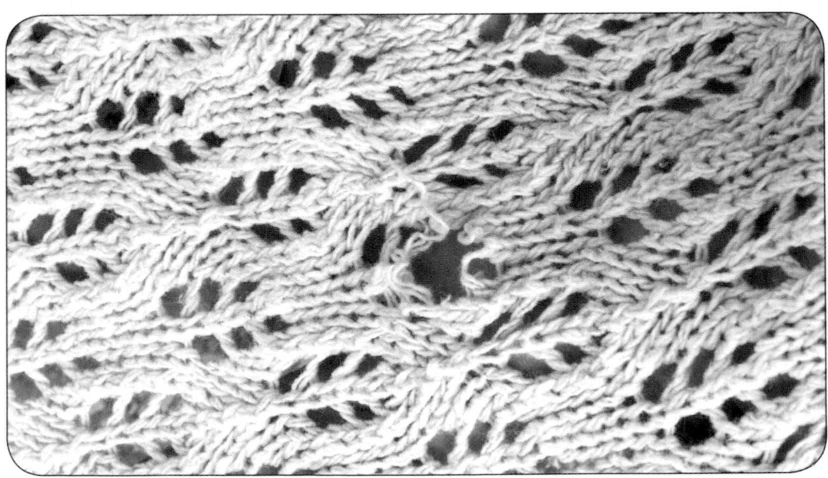

ABOVE Pulled threads can easily cause holes in knitwear. Use a crochet hook to draw the loose threads through the knitted stitches and repair the hole.

Question 73:
How do I mend a hole in a knitted garment?

First, check to see if any yarn strands have broken or torn. You will want to knot them or catch them with the needle to make sure they do not come out even more. You will be stitching from the inside with very fine yarn or thread that matches the sweater as best as possible.

If the hole is small, pull the edges together and then secure the thread at one end of the hole, on the wrong side. Stitch from side to side, picking a few threads of the knit on either side, to draw the edges of the hole together.

You also might be able to use a crochet hook to do some re-weaving, and then secure it at the edge with sewing thread. If the hole is big, you may well have to do some darning (see Question 74).

EXPERT TIP

“According to where the hole is you could be creative and add some decorative buttons, such as small pearl buttons, over the hole after mending and throughout the knit garment. Or try embroidering a flower over the hole and maybe on other areas of the sweater.”

Question 74:
How do I darn?

Darning is done with a simple running stitch in which the thread is taken back and forth across the hole in one direction, so that long stitches lie across the hole. The thread is then woven in and out of these long stitches in the opposite direction to repair the hole.

Pick a thread that is close to the colour and thickness of the item you want to darn. You can also use a dark colour for horizontal stitching and a lighter colour for vertical stitching. It doesn't have to match exactly if you are mending in a spot that no one will see; on the sole of a sock, for example.

Thread the needle with one or two strands of thread. Trim away any ragged edges without making the hole any larger. Secure the thread on the wrong side and bring the needle through to the right side. Sew a long stitch from one side of the hole to the other. Don't pull too tight; you want the thread and the garment to lie flat. Make long stitches back and forth until the hole is filled with parallel running stitches. Then, without cutting the thread, weave the needle in and out of the parallel stitches. Take a small stitch to secure the thread and then weave back across the parallel stitches; put the needle under those stitches you went over last time, and then over those you went under. Continue weaving in and out until the hole is covered.

EXPERT TIP

“ A darning egg is a hard egg-shaped instrument which is inserted into the toe or heel of a sock to hold the shape. When the repairs are finished, the darning egg is removed. Many of us may have seen a darning egg in our grandmother's sewing basket, but didn't know what it was. ”

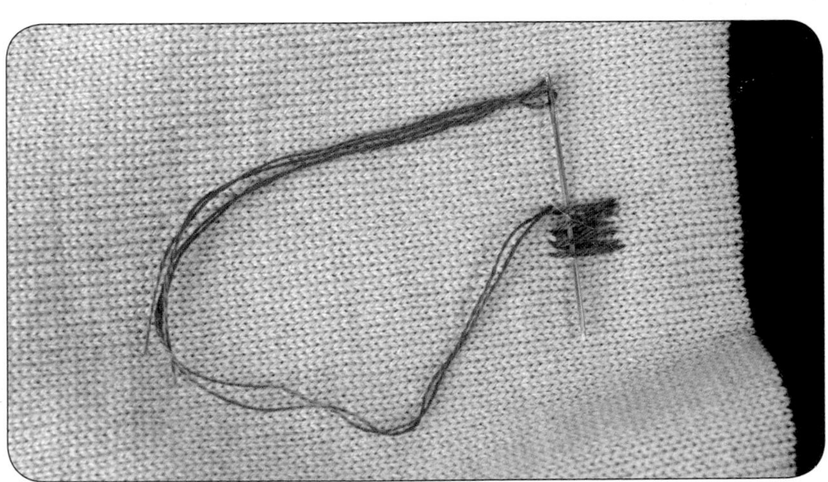

ABOVE After making long stitches across the hole in your knitted garment, weave the needle and thread in and out of these stitches.

Question 75: What kind of holes are suitable for patching?

The answer to this question can depend very much on your personal 'style'. Back in the 1960s, patches were in: everything was patched even if it didn't have a hole! Then styles changed and it became fashionable to just to wear the torn clothing – especially in blue jeans – with no patches. Now, anything goes.

Practically speaking, you probably do not want to patch a hole that is more than about 5cm (2in) square. First, you'll need to decide if the patch will go on the outside or inside of your garment. Patches that go inside the garment are usually just ironed on. However, with more wear and washing the hole will probably continue to fray and need to be trimmed, showing the patch a little more each time it is trimmed. But, if you do not want the patch to show, this is your best bet.

The most frequent place on a garment that will need a patch is the knees of children's pants, since they spend a lot of time kneeling while they are playing.

ABOVE Because jeans are made of such a long-lasting fabric, they are often worn for longer than other garments and so can develop frayed areas that may need patching.

Question 76:
Where can I get patches?

Ready-made patches can be purchased in any sewing or craft store, or haberdashery department. You can also buy them from online sewing suppliers. Even drug stores and grocery stores may have some packages of emergency patches.

You can buy sew-in patches but the greatest range available are the iron-on sort. These come in many different thicknesses and sizes; you can also buy pieces of iron-on fabric or iron-on tape that you can cut to the size required. There are many different colours available, including denim. Sew-in patches are necessary when you can't iron the item to be patched; you'll find sew-in patches for suede and vinyl on sale.

ABOVE Iron-on patches come in a wide range of sizes and colours. Buying larger ones can be practical, since you can cut several smaller patches from one.

Question 77:
Can I make my own patches?

You can buy iron-on patches and appliqués in all different shapes, sizes and colours; however, you may wish to make your own patch. If the garment you are patching is made of a fabric that can take high levels of heat and steam (test it first, using a pressing cloth), then you can use fusible webbing to create your own patch. Fusible webbing is a man-made, nylon-fibre mesh that melts with the heat of the iron to fuse two layers of fabric together. You iron the fusible webbing onto a piece of fabric, and then you can iron that piece of fabric onto another material.

Fusible webbing is available in various weights. Use the weight that is closest to the fabric you will be fusing. For patches, you can use the heavier weights. However, be careful; the glue from the webbing may seep through the fabric leaving a melted mess and it is difficult to sew through. Heavy weight fusible webbing will also gum-up a sewing machine needle or any regular sewing needle.

To make your own iron-on patch, choose a fabric that will not fray easily and try to match the patch-fabric weight to the garment-fabric weight. For example, if you are patching denim jeans you can usually use heavier fabric; however, if you are patching a cotton summer dress, use a lighter weight fabric. Cut a piece of fabric that is bigger than you need to start and then fuse a similar size piece of the webbing to the wrong side of this, following the manufacturer's instructions.

Once the fabric and webbing are fused together, trim to the size required for your patch. It is better to do this after the fusing process so you can be sure that the reverse of the patch is completely covered by the fusible webbing.

Question 78:
How do I attach a patch to a garment?

To attach a patch to a garment you need to first decide whether the patch will go on the inside or outside. Obviously, the patch will show on the outside, but patches can add to the fashion of a garment and with children's clothes, patches can certainly add some fun and creativity.

If you have purchased a shop-bought patch, trim it to about 1cm ($^3/_8$in) larger all round than the hole; the same applies to any patches you have made (see Question 77). If you have purchased a sheet of patching fabric, cut out either a circle or a rectangle with rounded corners. Patches with rounded corners will stay on much better; points usually start peeling off after a few washings.

First, trim off any little threads that are fraying around the patch. Follow any directions that came with your shop-bought patch or with the fusible webbing (if you are making your own patch) to iron the patch in place. Whatever the settings given for your iron, remember to test this on a hidden area of the garment first. Most iron-on patches and webbing use a fairly high heat. It is a good idea to use a pressing cloth, because you will be pressing the patch down for a few minutes at a time. Once the patch is set, let it cool. If the directions have been followed correctly, the patch should stay on for many washings. However, to guarantee the patch will not begin to peel off and to add a decorative look, you may wish to stitch around it.

LEFT If you're patching a pair of children's trousers, you could use a different coloured fabric for the patch and make a feature of it.

Question 79:
How do I sew on a home-made patch or add decorative stitching?

Cut your decorative fabric slightly larger than the hole that needs patching, plus 5mm (¼in) to turn under the edge. Your patch can be simply square or round; or you can cut out a more decorative shape, like a heart. Turn under the raw edges of your shape by 5mm (¼in) and tack in place. Pin or tack the patch in position over the hole.

You can sew the patch down so that the thread does not show on the right side. Thread your needle with single thread and knot; secure the thread on the wrong side and bring the needle to the right side. Work round the patch using slip stitch (see Question 42). If you want to use a decorative stitch, then try blanket stitch (see Question 44). Use either double thread, embroidery floss or a thin yarn so the stitches really show. If you use thicker thread, you will probably need a larger needle with a larger eye. Make sure that the needle can easily slip through the fabric.

When you have sewn all the way around the patch, overlap a few stitches, pull the needle to the inside of the garment, knot the thread and cut.

EXPERT TIP

“A reminder – you do not need to have a hole to add a patch or appliqué to your garment. You can patch or appliqué simply for decoration!”

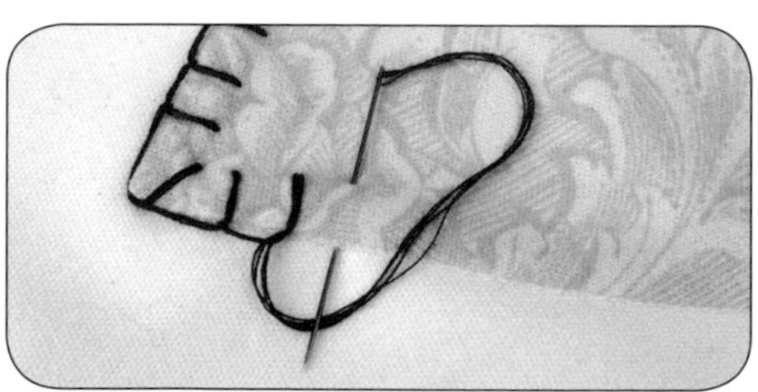

LEFT Turn under the edges of your patch and work blanket stitch all round to secure in place and add a decorative touch.

Question 80:
What should I know about seams?

A seam is formed when you bring two layers of fabric together and join them by stitching along one or more edges. The seam allowances are the width of the fabric from the raw edge to the stitching line. In home dressmaking, the seam allowance is generally 1.5cm (5⁄8in). In ready-made garments this is usually less, to save on fabric.

What distinguishes one seam from another is the method used to finish the raw edges of the seam allowance. In the most basic of seams, the edges are left unfinished. This, however, is only really an option on fabrics that don't fray; virtually all ready-made garments will have some sort of seam finish.

Most seams are finished with a type of oversewn stitching; each seam allowance might be oversewn separately, or both allowances might be oversewn together. Some seams, especially those that need to lie flat, are stitched down and this stitching shows on the right side of the garment as topstitching.

Highly tailored garments will have the neatest seam finishes of all. In French seams, the seam is stitched so that the raw edges are enclosed within a second seam. In Hong Kong seams, the edges of the seam allowance are hemmed. And in certain couture garments, you might find the seam allowances bound with tape.

ABOVE In garments made from thick fabrics, the seams are usually stitched down – with topstitching visible on the right side – to help them lie flat.

Question 81:
What are the different types of seam finishes?

To be able to fix a ripped seam or even rip out, alter and re-sew a seam, it would be helpful to know a little bit about each type of seam finish. The seam and seam finish methods chosen by the manufacturer (and home stitcher) are usually a matter of preference, based on the type of fabric and where the seam is located. For example, a seam down the side of a skirt would be finished in one way and the seam in a neckline may be finished in another way for comfort reasons. Also, if a garment is lined, sometimes the seams are not finished off.

Overlocked seams are sewn and then the raw edges of seam allowance are oversewn (overlocked) together, then pressed to one side. Most seams are finished this way. In an open seam, each raw edge of the seam is oversewn separately and seam allowances are pressed open.

In a topstitched seam, the seam is sewn and the seam allowances serged, before being pressed to one side and then topstitched about 1cm (3⁄8in) in from the seam to make a particularly strong seam.

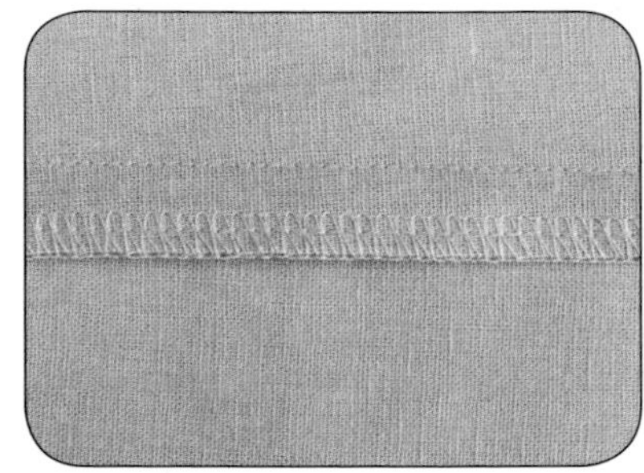

ABOVE Overlocked seam (wrong side).

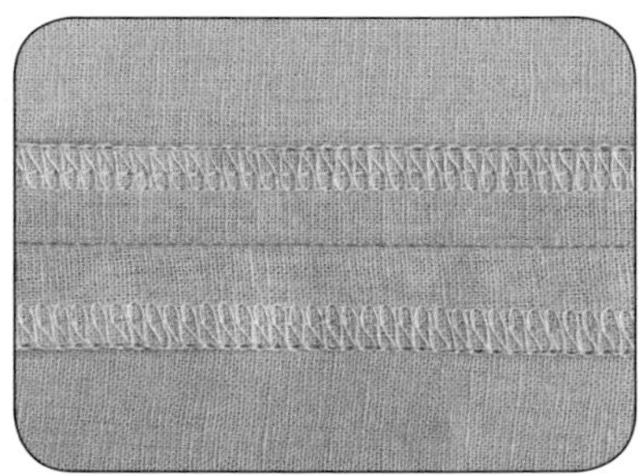

ABOVE Open seam (wrong side).

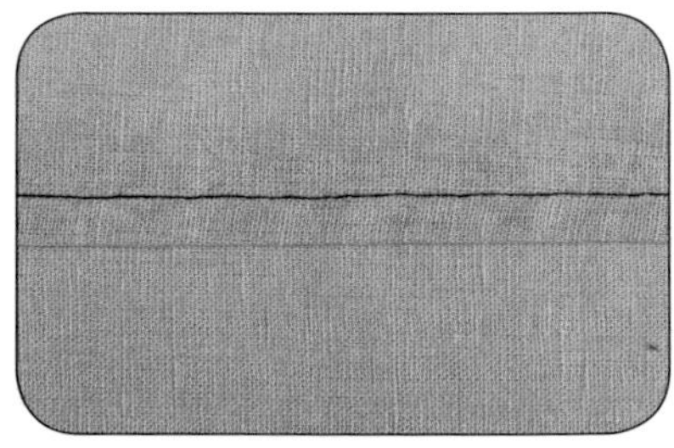

ABOVE Topstitched seam (right side).

Question 82:
How can I fix a ripped seam?

Fixing a ripped seam depends on how the seam is sewn and finished. Whichever seam and seam closure was chosen, the task is still quite simple and can usually be done in a matter of minutes, although there are a few seams where a rip should be fixed with a sewing machine. This includes where several joining seams have ripped open, such as at the underarm and sleeve seams, or at sleeve and shoulder seams.

It's frustrating to find a hole or tear in one of your favourite garments, especially right when you plan to wear it, but often you can fix the rip or hole with simple mending or patching. If you have never done this before, don't fear; it's not as hard as it sounds. The type of edge finishing determines how the seam will be mended.

ABOVE It only takes one thread to break in a seam for the rest of the stitching to pull out.

Question 83:
What are the methods to fix a tear in each seam closure?

Mend overlocked and open seams using backstitch (see Question 43). This is the strongest of the hand stitches and it looks very much like machine stitching when done neatly.

Since you are working on the inside of your garment, you do not need to hide the thread knots. Turn the garment inside out and find the broken stitches. If you are working on open seams, bring the allowances together. If you are working with overlocked seams, the two allowances will already be together. Thread a needle with a single strand of matching or slightly darker coloured thread. Knot the thread. Begin in the original stitching line about 2.5cm (1in) to the right of where the seam is ripped. Then work backstitch along the seam allowance to about 2.5cm (1in) beyond the ripped section. Do not pull the thread too tight; you want the resulting seam to be free of puckers. As always, practise the stitch before you sew your garment. Finish by knotting the thread.

Mending a topstitched seam is rare, since these seams are usually found on denim where extra thick thread is used; they rarely rip. If you need to, you can use the slip stitch explained in Question 42. The seam edges are sewn down for decorative purposes, but also so that the stress is taken away from the seam area. You will not be able to separate the seam allowance from the garment; therefore, carefully pick up only a few fibres of the fabric instead of going all the way through to the right side of the garment. This will be much easier in denim. Make sure that you follow the old seam line

ABOVE On topstitched seams, work slip stitch along the ripped area of seam on the right side of the garment.

exactly and that the thread does not show through on the right side of the fabric. Using the exact colour or slightly darker thread will help keep the thread hidden.

If the seam allowances are difficult to get to (for example, if a lining is sewn to the garment), you can use the slip stitch (see Question 42) on the outside (right side) of the garment. Thread your needle with single thread and knot it. Make sure that the thread colour matches and your stitches stay tiny. You can also use slip stitch on the right side of heavier knits, such as sweaters. Using the slip stitch on sweater knits will make the stitching 'invisible'. Begin about 2.5cm (1in) from where the seam began to rip and work slip stitch. Each stitch goes into the fold, comes out, and goes straight across into the opposite fold. This way, when the thread is pulled tight, it 'disappears' into the sweater knit. Continue from side to side to about an inch beyond where the seam has ripped. Finish by pulling the thread to the wrong side, knotting and cutting the thread.

Question 84:
My pockets always rip from keeping too much change in them; can they be fixed?

Thread your needle with a double thread and knot the end. Since the pocket does not show, it doesn't really matter what colour thread is used, however most internal pockets are white or beige so you might as well use that colour since it's one of the spools you should always have. Using backstitch (see Question 43), stitch round the seam, following the line of the old stitching. Fasten off securely.

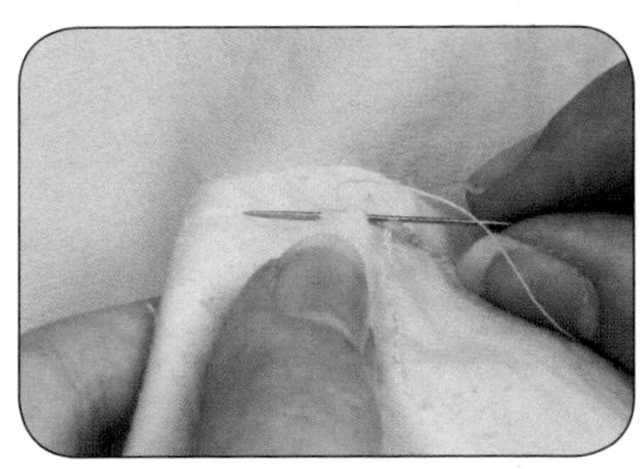

ABOVE Backstitch round the rip in your pocket to sew up the hole. Finish off neatly and trim off any loose threads that remain.

Question 85: What types of hems are there and how wide should hems be?

Like everything else, there are several types and widths of hems – they all depend on the dressmaker or manufacturer, and the type of fabric and style of the garment. For example, wools and other heavier fabrics usually have deeper hems, whereas knits usually have very shallow hems.

Hems are sewn by several methods. Most popular are hems sewn down by a sewing machine, with the stitching showing on the right side of the fabric. Hems can also be blind-stitched by machine, where the stitching is about 5mm (¼in) below the edge of the hem and no stitching shows on the right or wrong side of the garment. On overlocked blind hems, the edge of the hem is finished and then the hem is blind stitched by machine.

ABOVE Tailored trousers made from heavier weight fabrics such as wool will have deeper hems.

Question 86:
How do I take the hem down on ready-made garments?

Once again, I'll be using the term 'rip out' to discuss letting down a hem. But remember, ripping means carefully taking out the stitches in a hem and not actually ripping. No matter how experienced you are at sewing everyone rips out, even fashion professionals.

Slide the point of the seam ripper (see Question 35) under one of the stitches on the hem and cut the thread. Do this every few stitches. Then gently tug at the stitches to pull out a few inches of the hem. Keep doing this around the hem.

LEFT You can use a seam ripper to both cut the stitches on a hem and to pull them out.

EXPERT TIP

“When ripping out stitches, you will ultimately have a lot of little threads all around. One of the best ways to clean up is to take sticky lint roller, or just a wide piece of masking tape, and pat the garment and whatever surface you were just working on, and your own clothes, with the roller.”

Question 87:
How do I prepare a skirt or trousers for hemming?

What normally needs to be done to prepare a garment for hemming is to take down the old hem and then pin up the new one.

After ripping out the old hem (see Question 86), press the old hem crease out. Then try on the garment, standing on a flat surface (preferably not on a carpet), wearing the same belt and shoes you will wear with the trousers or skirt. Sometimes it's easier to stand on a stool and have someone else measure and pin. You then need to turn under the hem to where you think you might like it and pin it in place. It may take a few tries, testing different lengths to get the right garment length.

It's important to do all these things. Not pressing out the old crease, not wearing a belt or wearing shoes that are higher or lower than the ones you intend to wear with the garment can all effect the final hem length and your hem may turn out too long or short.

EXPERT TIP

“It's important to wear the same belt when you try on trousers or skirts that you intend to wear with the outfit. Belts lift up the back hem of the trousers or skirt slightly which will make a difference to the finished hem.”

Question 88:
How do I turn up a hem in trousers, skirts or dresses?

Once you have decided on where you want the new hem (see Question 87) and pinned it up, place pins exactly along the fold of the hem, spacing them 5–7.5cm (2–3in) apart. These pins will mark the foldline of the new hem.

Decide on how deep you want the hem. Measure from the new foldline up the hem allowance to the amount you've decided on for the depth; mark this with chalk. Trim away the excess fabric.

If you are changing the hem quite a bit you may be able to cut off the entire original hemmed section, but if you are changing it only a small amount you will need to rip out the original stitching first to create a large enough hem allowance. Trim the seam allowances within this hem allowance to 5mm (¼in) to reduce bulk.

Remove the marker pins along the foldline and press the fold in place, using a pressing cloth. Remove one or two of the pins holding the hem in place and start turning under the raw edge of the hem, pinning the hem back down as you go. Continue all the way round the hem until the edge is completely turned under and the hem is pinned in place.

Try on your garment once more to check the length and to make sure it is all even. Take off the garment and turn inside out. Baste along the hem to hold it in place. You are then ready to stitch the hem down – see Question 89.

LEFT Once the hem is turned up and pressed in place, you need to turn under the raw edges and pin to secure.

Question 89:
What stitches do I use to hem?

After you have prepared your hem (see Question 87) and turned it up and tacked it in place (Question 88) it is time to sew. Thread a needle with a single thread and knot the end. Working on the wrong side, secure the thread in the edge of the hem and work hemming stitch (see Question 40) along to the end.

To secure the thread at the end of a row of stitching or when a new strand of thread is needed, simply knot the thread and tuck the end into the hem of the garment. Another way to knot the thread is to stitch in the same place a few times, going through the same thread loop.

> EXPERT TIP
>
> **“If you run out of thread in the middle of stitching a hem, restart your stitching about 2.5cm (1in) before where you left off. This overlap will make the hem extra secure just in case the knot pulls through.”**

Question 90:
What do I do if the hem circumference is very wide?

Many skirts and trousers are much wider at the hem, which means that they will be wider at the edge of the hem than at the foldline. In order to to hem garments like this, you will need to ease in excess fabric.

After you have measured the hem, pin it at the hem fold. Doing this will keep the hem in place as you ease in the extra fabric. You could tack along the fold if preferred. You then need to pin up the rest of the hem, turning under the raw edge at the same time, and ease in the extra material. Work around the hem, pinning it up and taking little pleats in the hem allowance as you go. Be careful not to make each gather too large or too small. Pin through each little pleat to hold it in place. Make sure the pleats are evenly spaced around the circumference of the hem. If you wish, you could tack around the hem, to hold the pleats in place. If you do, make sure you tack through all the layers of fabric.

Try on the trousers before you start to sew. Once you are happy with the hem, begin stitching using the hemming stitch (see Question 40). Make sure you make stitches through all the layers of the pleats. (If liked, you can stitch the pleats down with slip stitch after hemming.) Every so often, turn the garment over to the right side and check that everything is lying as flat as it can be before pressing. Continue to do this all the way around the hem.

When you are finished sewing the hem, take all the pins out. Before knotting and cutting the thread, pull gently on the hem horizontally to smooth out any bunching. Again, check the right side of the garment. When you've finished stitching, press the garment on the wrong side using a pressing cloth.

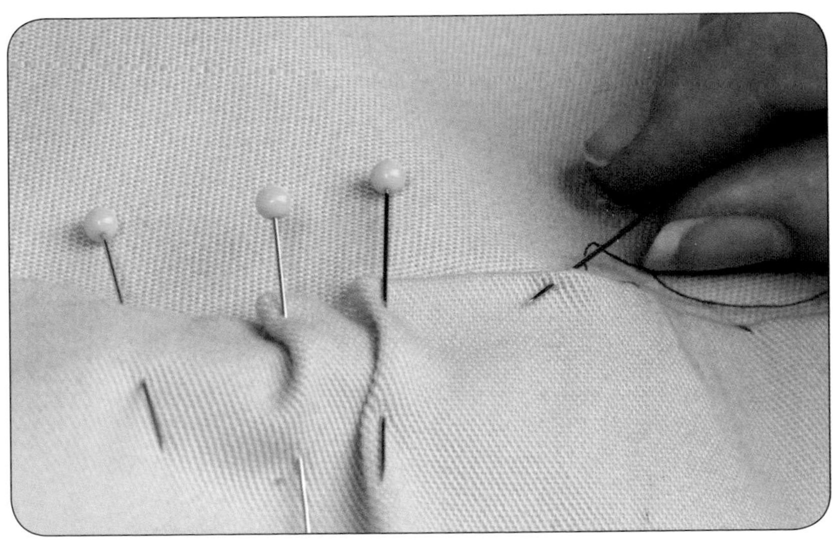

ABOVE Pin neat pleats in place before working hemming stitch around your hem.

Question 91:
What do I do if the hem circumference is very narrow?

Many garments will become more narrow or tapered towards the hem, especially trousers. If you turn up a new hem in such a garment, you will need to open out the seam in the hem area if you want the hem to be smooth. Turn up your hem to the length desired and then rip out the stitches of one or both of the seams in the hem allowance only, until the hem lies flat. Turn under the sides of the split seam and pin in place. Slip stich the edges to the seam allowances, being careful that the stitches do not go through to the right side of the garment. Hem stitch the rest of the hem in place.

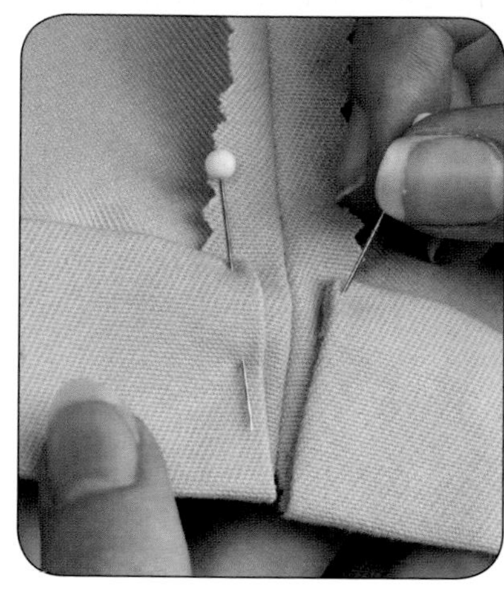

ABOVE After opening out the seam at the hem edge, turn under the seam allowances and pin in place. Then stitch to secure.

Question 92:
How do I hem the lining?

Linings are hemmed the same way as the garment fabric, except the lining should be 4–5cm (1½–2in) shorter than the garment so when you sit down or move your arm, the lining will not show. Hems in linings face opposite the garment hem, meaning that the insides of both garment and lining face each other. If you have a sewing machine available, you can sew the lining by machine, since the stitching will not show. Otherwise, hem by hand as explained in Question 89.

Question 93:
How do I mend a frayed hem?

There are several ways to mend a frayed hem. The simplest way would be to take the hem up about 5mm (¼in). However, if this will make the garment too short for you, you can try a few other methods.

Try trimming away any threads and then use Fray Check or a clear nail varnish on the hem edge to stop further fraying.

Another method is to cover the frayed edge with binding. Let down the hem and sew bias binding around the edge of the hem 5–10mm (¼–½in) from the frayed edge. Turn it over the frayed edge and stitch in place. Then re-hem by stitching into bias tape. Alternatively, unpick the hem and machine stitch a length of ribbon or narrow lace to the edge of the hem, just below the fraying. Turn up the hem again and hem stitch around the edge of the ribbon or lace.

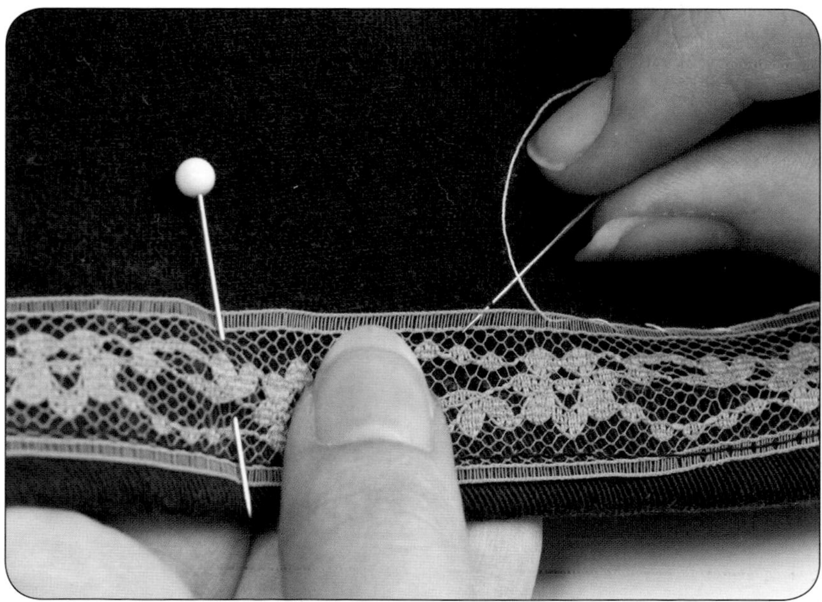

ABOVE Unpick your frayed hem and then stitch some lace around the edge. Turn up the hem and hem stitch into the edge of the lace.

Question 94:
Can I make the hem of my trousers longer at the back for when I wear heels?

If you intend to always wear high heels with a certain pair of trousers, then hemming them so the back is slightly longer will make the trousers look nicer.

Prepare the trousers in the same away as instructions in Question 87. When you are preparing for the hem (and possibly cutting), measure the hem 2.5cm (1in) longer for the back. Remember to pin up and try on the trousers wearing your shoes (and a belt if you plan to wear the trousers with one).

Fold and pin the centre front of the hem where it was previously measured. Then fold up the centre back of the trouser leg's hem. The difference between the front centre and back centre should never be more than 2.5cm (1in). Fold up the rest of the trouser hems, tapering from front to back for a smooth hem edge. The side seams should be exactly half of the amount between the front centre and back.

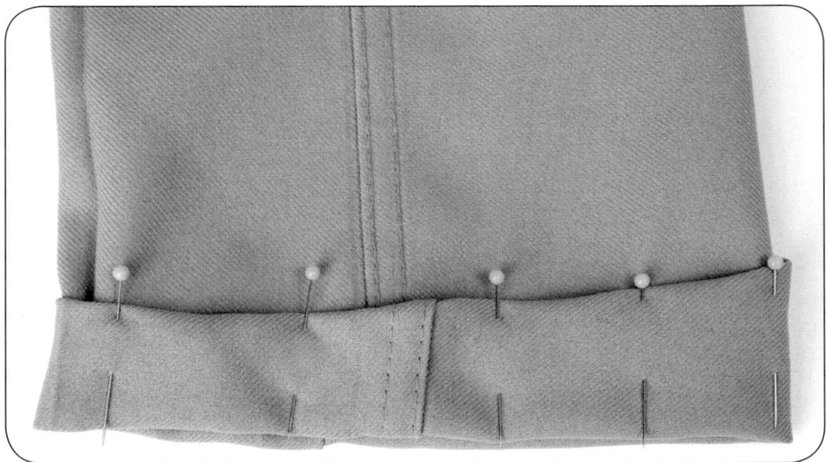

ABOVE To adjust pants to wear with high heels, you need to pin up the hem so that the hem is deeper at the back than at the front.

Question 95:
How do I hem leather?

Garments made of leather are expensive to buy and so if the hem comes down you will want to fix it rather than discard the clothing. Anything made of leather has been sewn with a special industrial sewing machine and with special thread. And certain areas will have also been glued in place.

If you have a hem come down on leather pants, skirt or jacket, first look and see if the hem has been stitched or glued in place. If it has been stitched and the original stitching holes are visible, you could try re-sewing the hem in place by hand (it's unadvisable to use your sewing machine since it's not designed to sew leather and you may break it).

Thread your needle with double thread or topstitching thread and draw it through some beeswax (see Question 13); this will make it easier to pull the thread through the leather. Turn the garment to the wrong side. Find some existing stitches along the hem that are still secure and insert your needle underneath. Pull the thread through until there's a short length left and then knot the thread around the existing stitches. Insert your needle in one of the holes left by the missing stitches and draw the thread through to the right side. Then stitch along the hem, following the old stitch holes. Take the thread to the wrong side to finish, and knot it to an existing stitch. If the old holes aren't visible, or are too small for your needle, then don't attempt to stitch the hem. It's very hard to handstitch leather so this is one to leave to the tailor.

However, you could use a special leather glue and glue the hem back in place, especially if the hem was glued originally. There is a glue made specifically for leather that remains flexible when dry. Follow the manufacturer's directions carefully and apply adhesive to both surfaces to be bonded. When the surfaces are tacky, press the two layers together. Use weights or books to hold the layers together while they dry. An important thing to remember when mending leather, is not to iron it.

96 How do I choose a sewing machine?

97 How do I use a sewing machine?

98 What accessories and needles would I need for my machine?

99 What sort of thread should I use?

100 What additional supplies do I need for use with my sewing machine?

101 How do I rip out a machine-stitched seam?

102 How do I rip out overlocked seams?

103 If I need to take a garment apart, what are all the parts and pieces?

104 Why would I need to know this?

105 What is interfacing?

106 What is lining and underlining?

107 What is seam binding?

108 What is bias binding?

109 Can I make my own binding?

5
MACHINE-SEWING KNOW-HOW

Question 96:
How do I choose a sewing machine?

Sewing machines differ mainly in the amount of different types of sewing you can do with them. Unless you plan to be sewing quite a bit, a basic, good quality machine with several standard stitches – straight, zigzag, buttonhole and possibly special stitches for knit fabrics – should be enough. Ninety-nine percent of sewing machines have all these stitches; the more complex (and expensive) machines offer a much wider range of stitches. Many newer machines are computerised; however for someone just beginning to machine sew, I would recommend starting with a reliable, yet simple sewing machine. You can even consider buying a re-conditioned second-hand model, or even borrow one!

To do the mending and alterations in this book, you will be fine with a basic machine, as long as it does straight and zigzag stitches, and has attachments for doing zips and buttonholes. A computerised machine may be an option if you are considering spending more time and effort on sewing. At some time in the future, most sewing machines will be computerised so you may want to start with one.

Question 97:
How do I use a sewing machine?

First of all, you must read the owner's manual that comes with your sewing machine and familiarise yourself with its various parts and capabilities. That said, most electric sewing machines (not the new computerised ones though) are operated in the same general way.

To begin using your machine, raise the needle to its highest position by turning the handwheel at the right of the machine. Make sure that the needle you are using is the correct size for the fabric you are sewing. Raise the presser foot. Thread the sewing machine and the bobbin following the guide in your owner's manual. Pull the top and bobbin threads to the back of the machine's needle and foot. Insert your fabric underneath the raised presser foot and position the point where you want to start stitching under the needle. Lower the presser foot on to the fabric and move the machine handwheel toward you until the needle pierces the fabric. To begin stitching, press on the foot pedal. Gently guide the fabric as it is pulled to the back of the machine, following as accurate a stitching line as possible. Don't push or pull the fabric through. End stitching by raising the needle to its highest position. Raise the presser foot and pull the fabric out and to the left. Cut the bottom and top threads to release the fabric.

EXPERT TIP

"Take care not to let your fingers get under the needle of the machine as it is running. Take it from me – it hurts!"

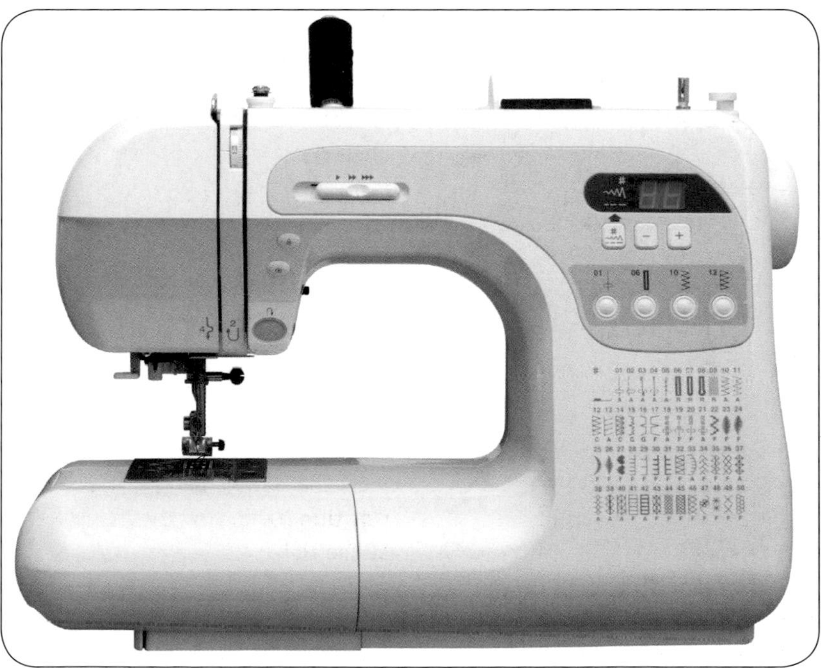

ABOVE Although they look complex at first, most sewing machines are simple to thread and operate; just follow instructions in the owner's manual.

Question 98:
What accessories and needles would I need for my machine?

All sewing machines come with some accessories, some with more than others. As long as your sewing machine has the basic stitches mentioned in Question 96, you should not need to buy any more accessories; the attachments that come with your machine should be adequate to complete the mending and alterations covered in this book.

Your machine will also come with a variety of needles. However, you may need or want to purchase more at some stage; needles do wear out and break sometimes, and you may need a special sized needle for sewing a certain fabric. Needles come in many different sizes and types according to the fabrics being sewn.

Understanding the size numbering associated with sewing machine needles will help you make the correct choice and avoid problems with your sewing machine. The European system of numbering machine needle sizes uses 60 to 120, with 60 being a fine needle and 120 being a thick, heavy needle. American sizes range from 8 to 19; 8 being fine and 19 being thick. Machine needles are often labelled using both systems; the average needle size is 75/11. If you look very closely at your sewing machine needles you will see the size stamped on the end that you insert in the sewing machine. It is very small and you may well need a magnifying glass to be able to read the information!

You should keep a variety of needle sizes among your sewing supplies. When you fit a different sized needle for a specific project always test it and the thread you've selected on an unseen area or a scrap of material before stitching the actual garment.

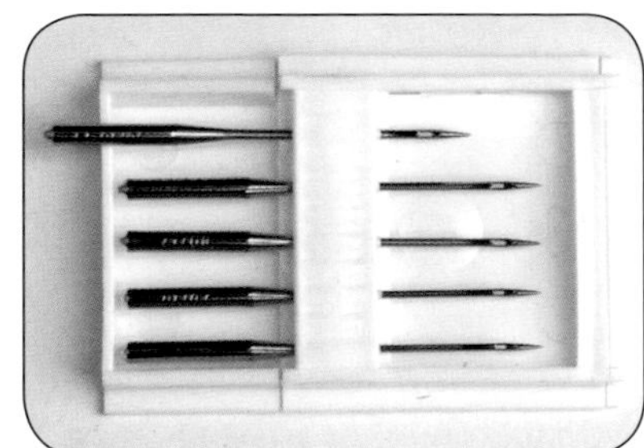

ABOVE You can buy packs of sewing machine needles in several sizes.

Question 99:
What sort of thread should I use?

There are many different threads for sewing on the market (see Questions 24 to 26). I would recommend that you do not purchase the really cheap threads for use on your sewing machine. You will find that the fluff and fuzz that comes off these threads needs to be cleaned out of your machine continually. And cheaper threads break more often than better quality ones, something that's very irritating while you're in the middle of sewing.

As you begin to sew more, you can buy specialty threads for your projects. However, they are not absolutely essential – the difference is similar to that between using a plain button and a decorative one. A good quality, polyester or cotton-wrapped polyester thread should be adequate for both top and bobbin thread in your machine.

Question 100:
What additional supplies do I need for use with my sewing machine?

Sewing machines can come with many attachments; feet to do cording, piping, blind stitching, zigzag, buttonhole, and so on. One machine I saw had 43 attachments!

However, to accomplish any of the instructions in this book, you will need only a basic machine. You need a straight-stitch foot and you may need a separate one for zigzag stitch – though many machines use the same foot for both stitches. You will need a zip foot and a buttonhole attachment.

It's important to keep your machine clean. Many come with a little brush for dusting out all the small crevices that seem to fill with fluff. Depending on the model and age of your machine, you may also need to oil it. You will probably get a small bottle of oil when you buy the machine, but make sure you buy the right sort when this runs out.

Question 101:
How do I rip out a machine-stitched seam?

When ripping out a machine-stitched seam you should do it with care. Remember, you are unpicking rather than ripping. As with ripping out a hem (see Question 86), you need to use a seam ripper (see Question 35). The seam ripper features a pointed end that you slip under a stitch. Behind the pointed end is a curved blade. As you push this against the stitch, it cuts through the thread.

To rip out a seam, turn the garment to the wrong side (if possible) and reveal the stitching along the seam in question. Use the ripper to cut three to four stitches, a few stitches apart. Pull gently until the thread on the other side of the seam begins to pull out. Carry on doing this until you have ripped out the area needed.

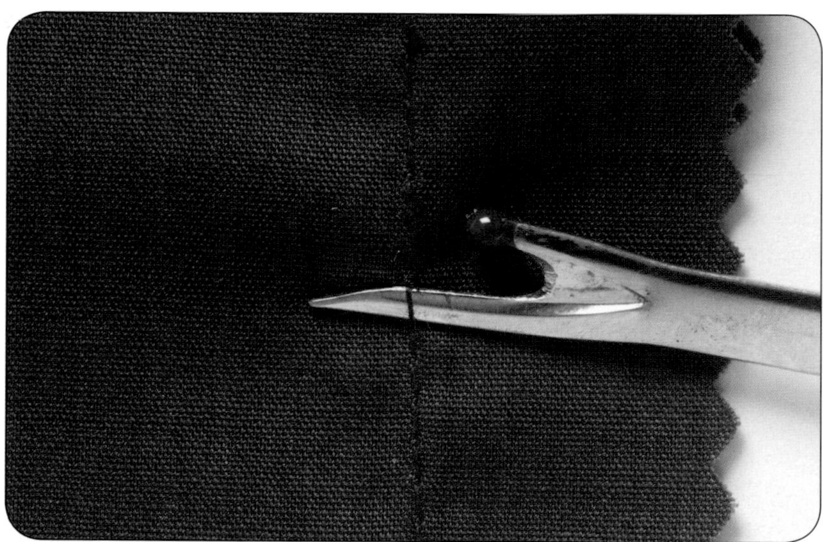

ABOVE Slip the seam ripper under a stitch and press it forwards gently to cut the thread. Do this at intervals along the seam and then tease out the unwanted stitches.

Question 102:
How do I rip out overlocked seams?

An overlocked seam has been created by a special sewing machine called an overlocker. This sews, trims and finishes the seam in one process. The allowances of the seam are oversewn together and form a strong, secure seam (see Question 81). Therefore, this type of seam can be a little trickier to rip out.

Think of overlocked stitches as a ladder, usually with two parallel 'poles' (but sometimes with just one) joined by many 'rungs'. The 'poles' are the straight stitching lines that run parallel to the seam edge; the 'rungs' are the oversewing that lie perpendicular to the stitching.

To rip out an overlocked seam, first cut stitches along the 'pole' or 'poles' for the area you want to rip out as described in Question 101. Then use the seam ripper to cut the 'rungs'. Do this in small sections, a few centimetres at a time – especially if you will be ripping out a large area of seam. Continue cutting the 'poles' and the 'rungs' in between until you have taken out the area of stitching for whatever mending needs to be done.

You will probably end up with lots of tiny bits of threads everywhere. Use a sticky lint roller (or just a wide piece of masking tape) to pick up all the little threads on your garment, your lap and the sewing area.

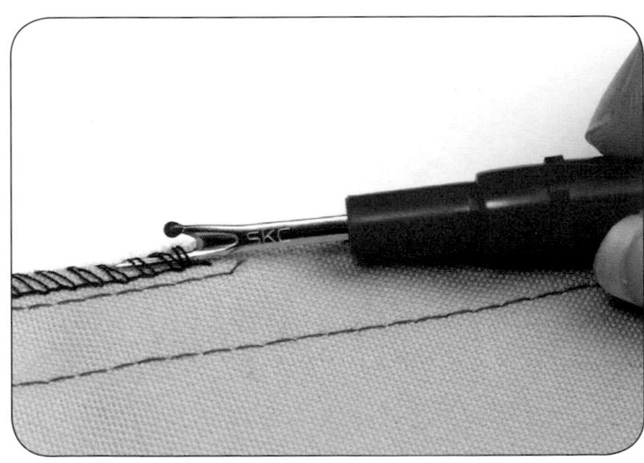

LEFT Use a seam ripper to unpick an overlocked seam, and work in small sections at a time.

Question 103: If I need to take a garment apart, what are all the parts and pieces?

This may sound like a simple question with a simple answer. However, how many people actually see garment pieces before they are all sewn together?

In a shirt or other top, the part touching your torso is the bodice. This is also the same in a dress; if a dress is made by joining top and bottom sections together, the top part is called the bodice. The front part of your bodice is, unsurprisingly, called the bodice front; the back is the bodice back. The holes for your arms are known as armscyes (though more commonly called armholes!); sleeves fit into the armscyes.

The neckline and wrist openings on garments are often finished with a collar and cuffs. On garments without collars and cuffs, these openings are finished with facings. To see the facings, look inside a garment; around the wrist or armhole opening (on a sleeveless garment), and around the neckline you will see a piece of fabric. This looks like a turned hem but it is, generally speaking, a separate piece of material stitched to the garment edge and turned in to the wrong side to finish the raw edges. You'll also see facings along the opening edges of buttoned shirts and blouses. And on jackets and coats, lapels are formed by stitching on facings and then turning the lapel section to the right side.

Facings are also sometimes used to finish the waistline of skirts and trousers instead of a waistband; this is known as a grown-on waistband. Skirts are generally formed of two parts – the skirt front and back – although some are made of just one piece of fabric, and the front and back may be divided into different sections. The legs of trousers are generally cut in two parts each – front and back – so each pair of trousers is made up of four leg sections. The back crotch seam is the join between the two back leg sections; the front crotch seam is the join between the two front leg parts. The inner leg seam is the join from the crotch, down the inside of the trouser legs, to the hem; the side seam is the join from the waist, down the outside of the trouser legs, to the hem.

Question 104:
Why would I need to know this?

Whether you are doing a repair or an alteration, if you have to take a garment apart – even if it's only a little bit – you should understand how that garment is constructed so you can put it back together again. You may need to unpick several parts of a garment seam and you may encounter several layers of fabric. If you know which bits are which you won't cut into the wrong parts, and you'll understand which areas will still be seen on the right side of your garment.

Question 105:
What is interfacing?

Interfacing is a textile used on the unseen or 'wrong' side of fabrics to make part of a garment more rigid. Interfacings can be used to stiffen or add body to fabric, such as the interfacing used in shirt collars; to strengthen a certain area of the fabric, for instance where buttonholes will be sewn; or to keep fabrics from stretching out of shape, particularly knit fabrics.

Interfacings come in a variety of weights and stiffness to suit different purposes. Generally, the heavier the fabric, the heavier the interfacing required. Most modern interfacings have heat-activated adhesive on one side to iron on. This type of interfacing is known as 'fusible' interfacing. Non-fusible interfacings must be sewn by hand or machine. There is also interfacing with stretch that was originally created to be used with knits, however it can be used for almost any type of fabric.

ABOVE Iron-on interfacing has the iron heat setting and timings marked on it.

Question 106:
What is lining and underlining?

Linings and underlinings are different types of fabric added to the inside of a garment; each with a different purpose. The lining is made up separately, as though it were a second garment and then stitched inside a garment, wrong side to wrong side. Its purpose is to cover up the details of the garment's construction and so gives a smoother and neater finish to the inside of clothing. Lined garments also have a neater, more tailored look from the outside. Linings can be used to protect the skin from rougher fabrics, such as in woollen garments. A lining can also help prevent the fabric of trousers bagging at the seat and at the knees, and prevent skirts from stretching and wrinkling. Lining also contributes to the ease of taking clothing on and off. Lining fabric is usually lightweight and sheer, such as silk, satin, sateen or the man-made equivalents.

Underlining is used to give more body to the fabric from which a garment is made. It's ideal, therefore, for reinforcing delicate materials. The garment fabric and underlining fabric are stitched together to make one layer from which the garment is then constructed. Underlining is generally a light- or medium-weight fabric and can be either soft or crisp in texture.

Question 107:
What is seam binding?

Seam binding does not stretch and is usually a single layer of fabric that is cut with the lengthwise or crosswise grain. It is used as a stabiliser for a seam that may stretch or tear easily, such as at an armhole or on the shoulder seam of a knit or t-shirt. It may also be used inside a garment to fold over the raw edges of a seam allowance to keep them from fraying, as in Hong Kong seams.

Question 108:
What is bias binding?

Bias binding is a tape that is used to bind the raw edges of fabric. This might be the raw edges of a seam or hem, or it might be the edges of a household item, such as a placemat, potholder, or quilt. It can be concealed, as in garment construction, or used as a decorative feature itself.

Bias binding is made by cutting fabric on the bias; in other words, the fabric has been cut across in a diagonal line, at a 45-degree angle to the grain. Fabric cut on the bias stretches, making bias binding invaluable for finishing curved edges and corners.

The strip of fabric cut for bias binding is turned under on both long sides; this turning is used when you stitch the binding in place. Shop-bought bias binding has the edges already turned and pressed; if you make your own, you will have to turn the edges under yourself. You can buy it in a range of different colours and patterns, and different widths, but it is surprisingly easy to make yourself (see Question 109).

To use bias binding, cut the length you require and then open out one folded edge. Pin the binding along the edge you want to finish, right sides together. Machine stitch in place, stitching along the fold line in the binding. Fold the binding over the fabric edge to the wrong side and pin in place. Slip stitch along the edge of the binding to secure.

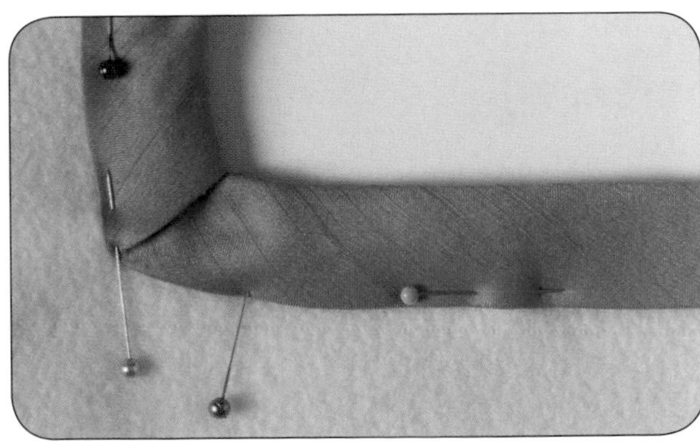

LEFT The stretch in bias binding makes it perfect for finishing corners.

Question 109:
Can I make my own binding?

You can make your own seam binding out of fabric which is the same as, or that coordinates with your project. To make straight seam binding, cut fabric strips three times the desired width along the straight edges of the fabric, following the grain or weave. Fold in half lengthwise and press. Fold the raw edges to the inside and press again.

To make bias binding, you will get the best results from a light- or medium-weight woven fabric. Cut the strips of fabric to four times the desired width. You can make bias binding any width you like but the narrower you cut the fabric strip, the harder it is to turn under the edges. It's recommended, therefore, that you cut the bias strips no smaller than 2.5cm (1in) wide. If you want a small piece of binding, then simply cut bias strips to the length required; remember, the bias is the true diagonal line across a piece of fabric. But if you need a long, continuous strip of bias binding, follow the method right.

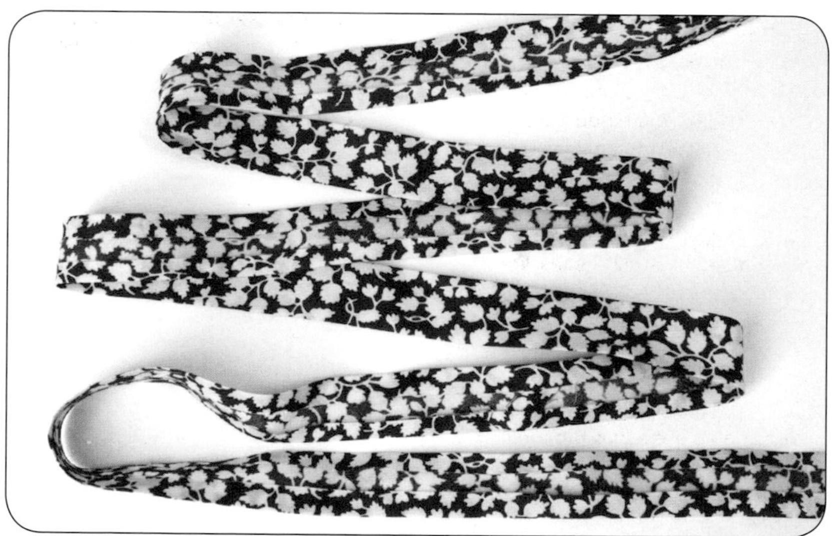

ABOVE If you make your own bias binding, you can pick a pretty patterned fabric that will add an element of decoration to your bound edge.

HOW IT'S DONE

- First cut a perfect square in your chosen fabric. Fold in half diagonally across the middle and press well to create an obvious crease.
- Unfold the fabric and then draw parallel lines on either side of the crease, spaced evenly apart and at least 2.5cm (in) distant. Cut off the corners of the fabric to make a new square, marked with the parallel lines (see top right).
- Take the two edges where the lines end and bring together, right sides of the fabric facing, so that the right-hand edge lines up with the first marked line in from the right (see bottom right). In other words, bring the edges together but offset by the depth of one marked line. Pin the edges together and machine stitch.
- You will have created a tube of fabric; the marked lines should spiral continuously around the tube. Press the seam open. Beginning at one end, cut continuously along the marked lines, cutting through the seam each time, to create one long bias strip.
- Turn under the long edges of the strip by 5mm (¼in) and press in place; or use a bias tape maker (a handy tool that turns the edges evenly) and iron to do the same job.

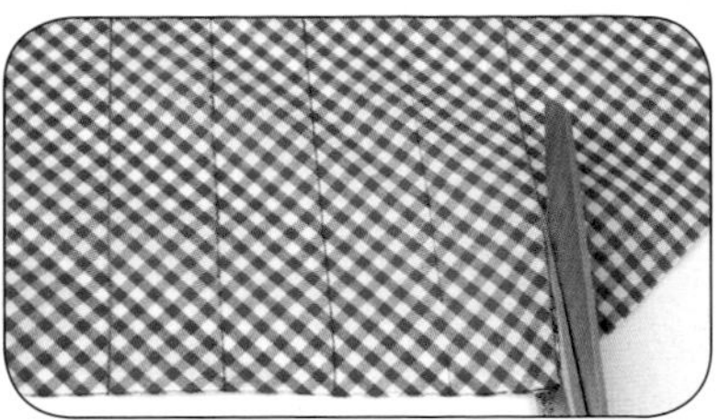

ABOVE Cut off the corners of your marked fabric to make a new square.

ABOVE Pin the edges together so that the lines you have drawn are offset to the depth made by one marked line.

110 What is ironing?

111 What is meant by pressing?

112 What is a pressing cloth?

113 What is a pressing ham?

114 How do I iron certain fabrics?

115 What is the best way to iron unusual or unknown fabrics?

116 How do I take out scorch marks?

117 Why does my iron keep spitting and how can I fix that?

118 How do I clean my iron?

6

IRONING AND PRESSING

Question 110:
What is ironing?

Most of us probably don't give ironing any thought; it's just another tedious chore that has to be done along with the rest of the laundry. And yet it plays an important part in our daily lives – there are very few people who would go out in crumpled and un-ironed clothing. Ironing is essential when it comes to making our clothes look good. In fact, proper ironing can revitalise garments. When you bring new clothes back from the shop they will often be crumpled after being packaged, so hang them up on a clothes hanger for a few hours to let the worst creases drop out and then iron into shape.

When a hot, usually metal, object is pressed on to creased fabric something happens to loosen the molecules in the material and straighten its fibres. Because there are many different fabrics with different kinds of molecular structure, there are different levels of heat needed to remove creases. Some fabrics, usually densely woven ones such as cotton, need great heat and even the addition of a little water in order to loosen the molecules. Others, with more open weaves, need only a moderate warmth to straighten the fibres.

Ironing plays an important role in sewing. If you're dressmaking, you won't get a good finish without ironing the pieces of your garment as you go. Similarly, when mending or altering clothes, you need to press anything you do to make sure the garments look as good as they did before.

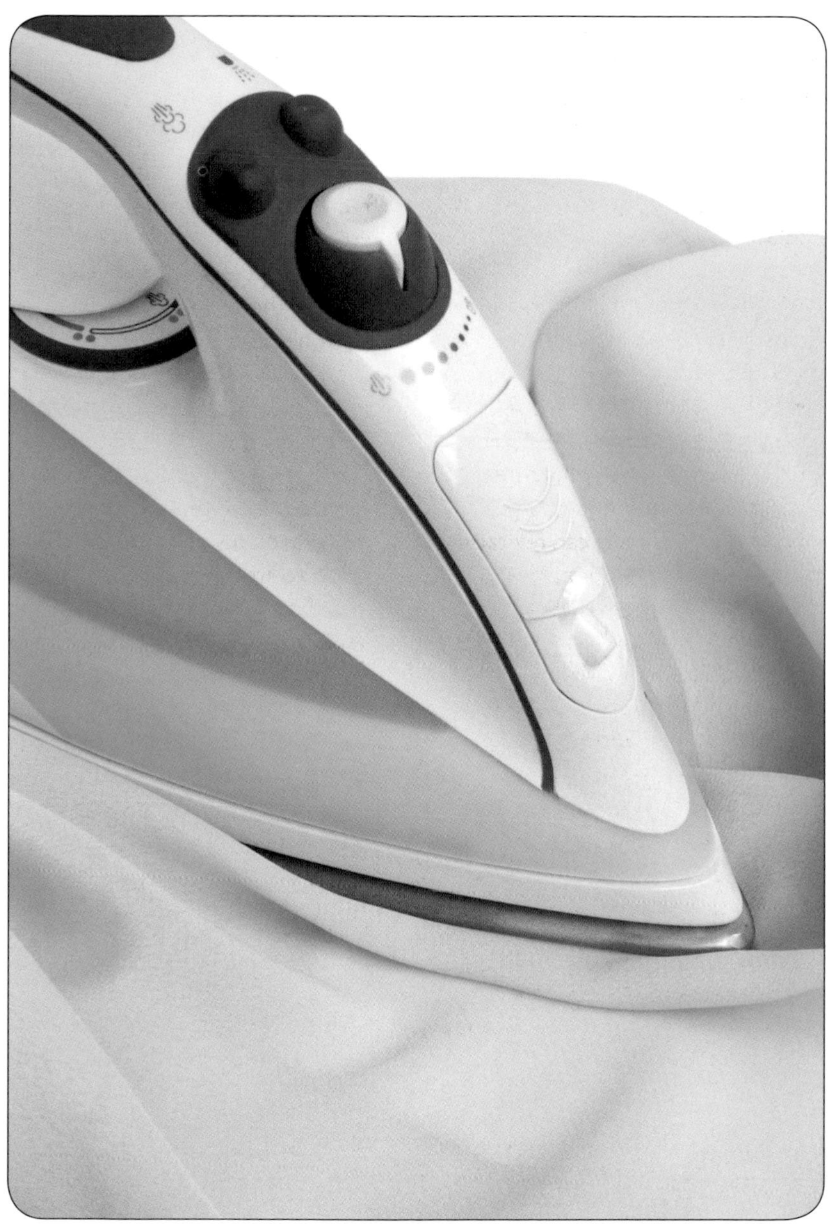

ABOVE Modern irons have a variety of different heat and steam settings to cope with the ironing needs of the wide range of different fabrics available today.

Question 111:
What is meant by pressing?

Pressing and ironing can be interchangeable terms. However, when talking about sewing and garment alteration, there is a subtle difference between the two functions. Pressing is done with a lifting and setting motion. It is used to flatten an area that has been stitched, like seams, darts, pleats, and hems. Pressing also means that you use a light touch of the iron. When you iron, you slide the iron back and forth more forcefully and with greater pressure.

To press successfully, always use a pressing cloth (see Question 112) placed over what you are pressing. Lay the iron on the cloth and over the seam, hem or whatever else you are pressing. Press gently and then lift up the iron. Sometimes a very gentle sliding motion can be used, but a combination of the heat setting, using steam, and a little bit of pressure should work.

EXPERT TIP

“Always test your ironing on an edge or seam allowance of your garment to make sure the iron setting is not too hot. Press on the wrong side of the garment whenever possible. Use the tip of the iron for small snug places that are hard to reach. To avoid press marks from the seam allowances, place a strip of brown paper between the seam allowances and the fabric before pressing. You should still use a pressing cloth.”

Question 112:
What is a pressing cloth?

A pressing cloth is simply a heat resistant fabric, such as cotton or silk, which does not heat up as quickly as the fabric you are ironing. Cotton pressing cloths prevent scorching or burning of the fabric being ironed. Delicate fabrics benefit from using a pressing cloth as they are sensitive to heat. Pressing cloths can also prevent a shine from developing on fabric after repeated ironing – synthetic fabrics pressed with a hot iron can sometimes produce a shiny look.

Cotton pressing cloths can be purchased from most hobby and sewing store retailers. However, it is easy to make your own from natural fibre fabrics. Cotton t-shirts that are 100 percent cotton and clean can be cut into a lightweight pressing cloth. Old cotton sheets or clean baby muslin squares can also be used. If a heavier pressing cloth is needed, 100 percent wool cloth can be used.

I personally use white or off-white silk organza because it is heat resistant and see-through, so you can see what you are ironing. Silk organza can be costly, but you only need a piece no more than 60cm (2ft) square and it will last for years. Silk organza will eventually turn yellow or brownish from the iron, but it still can be used.

LEFT A piece of cotton poplin makes an ideal pressing cloth. You don't need to finish the edges, but it's a good idea to wash it before use to rinse away lint.

Question 113:
What is a pressing ham?

A pressing ham is a tightly stuffed pillow that is used for pressing curved and difficult to reach areas. It is also known as a tailor's or dressmaker's ham. It gets its name simply because it is roughly the shape of a ham; one end is wider than the other.

To use a pressing ham, it is inserted into the garment and then the iron is used on that area. It's ideal for the proper pressing of sleeves, collars, zip plackets, long seams, small tucks and darts.

One side of the pressing ham is covered with wool; you should press fabrics that require low to medium iron temperatures on this side. The other side is covered with cotton for fabrics that can be ironed at higher temperatures.

ABOVE A pressing ham is a useful and relatively inexpensive item that helps you press any repaired or altered areas in hard to reach spots.

Question 114:
How do I iron certain fabrics?

You cannot iron all fabrics in the same way. Some are sturdier than others and can take more heat and greater pressure. Delicate fabrics need only the lightest of touches and the coolest temperature.

- Cotton is probably the easiest fabric to press. You can use either a dry iron or steam, and (usually) a high temperature setting. Be careful with cotton blends though; the other fibre used in the mix may require a lower temperature setting.

- Silk fabric should always be pressed with a dry iron – do not use steam. You can still use a fairly hot setting; but not as hot as for cotton.

- For wool, you can use plenty of steam to help shape the fabric. Alternatively, you can iron over a damp cloth.

- Linen can take a hot iron and steam, but iron it on the wrong side to avoid removing some of the shine found on this fabric.

- With blended fabrics, always use the iron setting for the fibre which has the lowest temperature.

- Take care when pressing fabrics with a nap. The 'nap' is the raised pile on a piece of material. Velvet has a distinct and obvious nap, but other fabrics may have a a shorter pile. Press on the wrong side whenever possible. If you must press on the right side, use a piece of the same napped fabric as a pressing cloth and put the two pieces nap sides together.

Question 115:
What is the best way to iron unusual or unknown fabrics?

The first advice here is to use a pressing cloth, especially if you are not familiar with the fabric contents. If there is no tag stating what the fabric content is, then start with the lowest setting on your iron and continue to increase the heat until you have the pressing results you want. When testing, try to find areas that will not show, just in case the iron is too hot.

Question 116:
How do I take out scorch marks?

If you iron a fabric at too hot a setting, or press for too long a time, you may find the fabric browning slightly. This means you have scorched it. Burn or scorch marks will look different on different fabrics. With man-made fabrics the scorched marks will look shiny because the fabrics are actually melting. Other fabrics may just become more matt; others may become dry and crisp.

If the fabric is badly burned and fibres are severely damaged, then you will not be able to get the mark out. Nor will you be able to if the fabric has melted. However, if the scorching is light and there is moderate discolouration there is something you can try.

Add a few drops of household ammonia to a few cups of water. Using a sponge, lightly rub the burned area, then rinse the area with clean water. Next time you iron, remember to use a press cloth.

Question 117:
Why does my iron keep spitting and how can I fix that?

As you iron and press garments and household linens, small fibres from the fabrics will be picked up in the holes of the sole plate. This lint then mixes with the steam and water in the iron and causes brown water to spit out from the holes. (The water is always brown; presumably this is because the fibres come from many different coloured fabrics and mingle in the iron to form brown!).

If you have a 'burst of steam' button on your iron, push that a few times after the iron has heated up and before you use it. You can also pour vinegar through the iron a couple of times to clean out the scale, (fill up the iron with vinegar, and turn it on to allow it to heat up and steam out the vinegar). Then, after it is cleaned out, fill the iron only with the type of water recommended by the manufacturer.

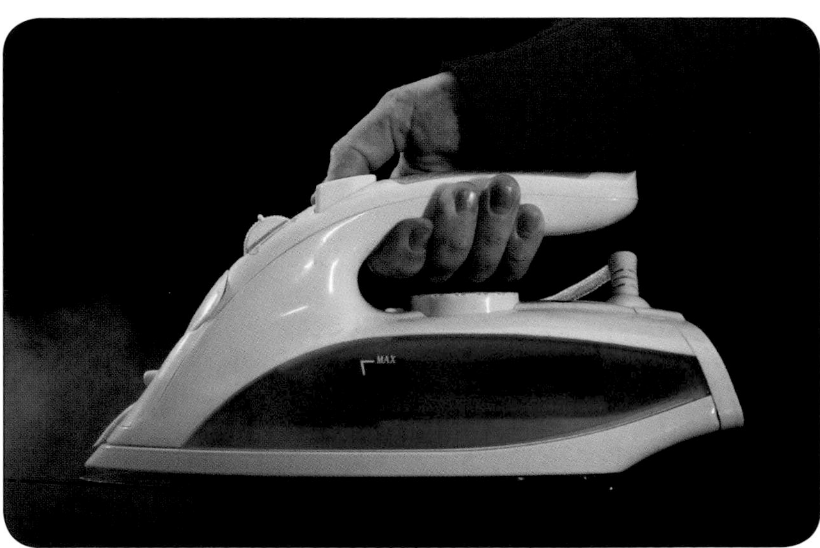

ABOVE If your iron starts spitting and brown water comes out of the sole plate, use your 'burst of steam' function to clear the vents.

Question 118:
How do I clean my iron?

Cleaning your iron on a regular basis is essential to maintaining your clothes, as well as the iron. Fortunately, cleaning the iron is no more difficult than cleaning most other small appliances. All it takes is a little bit of time and a few simple tools.

Place a small amount of a non-abrasive cleaner on a clean cloth and rub on to the sole plate until it is clean. (The sole plate is the flat metal part of the iron that you actually apply to your ironing.) Use pipe cleaners or cotton buds

LEFT If you iron something on too hot a setting, it can leave a deposit on the sole plate. Use a gentle non-abrasive cleaner or proprietary iron cleaner.

to clean out the sole plate steam holes. If using a proprietary brand of iron cleaner, check the directions on the packaging.

If it looks as though small deposits are being left in the small holes on the sole plate, the reservoir (where the water is kept) of your iron needs cleaning. Typically, the deposits are minerals from the water that you are using in the reservoir. The deposits may have a white colour which looks like salt. You will get more deposits in a hard-water area.

To clean the reservoir, fill it at least one fourth of the way up with white vinegar (the iron should be cold). Turn the iron on and place it on the steam setting. Steam iron a clean rag until the reservoir is completely empty.

Rinse the reservoir thoroughly with clean water by filling it completely and then emptying it completely. In order to avoid mineral build up and deposits, use distilled or purified water in the reservoir. If you use tap water, simply remember to clean the reservoir periodically.

Be careful, vinegar has a strong smell associated with it, especially when it is heated. Ventilate the area where you are working as much as possible, by opening windows, turning on vents or fans, or keeping the door open.

Cleaning the outside of the iron is also very important. Wipe the exterior clean with a damp cloth or sponge occasionally. If the iron does happen to pick up some form of residue on its exterior, then wipe it with a mild dish washing solution or a sole plate solution

When you are finished with the iron, you should always empty the reservoir and allow to dry out. This will also help to prevent mineral build up and lessen the frequency with which you need to clean the reservoir. Remember that the water in the reservoir may be very hot.

119 How can I alter an A-line skirt into a straighter skirt?

120 How can I alter an A-line skirt that is lined?

121 How can I take out some of the fullness in an elastic-waisted skirt?

122 How do I determine what needs to be fixed or altered on trousers?

123 What are my options?

124 How can I adjust the crotch depth?

125 How can I take in trouser legs if they are too baggy?

126 How can I turn long trousers into cropped ones?

127 How do I turn jeans into shorts?

128 How can I keep the faded-look hem on jeans but still make them shorter?

129 How do I do a French hem?

130 What is a dart?

131 How do I add a dart at the waist?

132 How do I put darts in an elasticated waistband?

133 How do I place elastic only in the back of the waistband?

134 How do I replace the old elastic in a waistband?

7

ALTERING SKIRTS AND TROUSERS TO FIT

Question 119:
How can I alter an A-line skirt into a straighter skirt?

Skirt styles seem to change every season. However, A-line skirts and straight-style skirts will most likely always be in fashion. If you have a skirt that is just too wide or a skirt that you wish to make straighter, it is quite simple to transform either.

First take the hem down by about 5cm (2in) at both side seams of the skirt that you will be taking in; iron the hem line out for those 10cm (4in) on each side. Try on the skirt inside out and pin the amount you wish to take in. If the skirt is not lined, you can try the skirt on and pin with the skirt inside out. If lined, it is best to pin with the skirt on properly.

Take in the same amount on both sides of the skirt. For an A-line skirt, you should begin to pin from the hip area down to the hem; begin with a very small amount – 2mm (1⁄16in) – and continue to take in more as you go down the seam. If the skirt has a side zip, begin pinning right under the zip and at the same place on the other side.

After the skirt is pinned evenly on both sides, walk around the room and sit down. This will make sure that you are not going to take in too much. If it is too tight when you sit down, move the pins outward but evenly.

If the skirt was pinned inside out, begin to sew exactly where your pins were placed; take out each pin before the needle goes over it! If the skirt was pinned on the outside, measure exactly how much each pin has taken in and re-pin on the inside of the skirt before sewing. Try the skirt on again before trimming any excess fabric and finishing the seams. Press the new seams open and rehem at the sides.

Question 120:
How can I alter an A-line skirt that is lined?

This is done in exactly the same way as described in Question 119, but the lining needs to be pulled away from the seams first. In a skirt, the lining is usually loose and can be pinned out of the way while you are taking the skirt in. Sometimes there may be a thread chain attaching the lining to the skirt. You can cut this where it is attached to the skirt and leave it hanging to the lining at this time. You can either trim this little chain off or reattach it to the skirt with a few little stitches after the skirt is rehemmed.

Take in the skirt as described in Question 119. You can also take in the lining the same amount that you took in on the skirt, but sometimes this may not be necessary. If it was a very full skirt and the lining is just as full, then the lining really should be taken in too, but if the lining is straighter than the skirt before alterations, then you may not need to touch the lining. (Of course if you are also hemming the skirt, then you'll need to hem the lining, too).

ABOVE Skirts made in heavier weight fabrics are generally lined. So if you're taking in a woollen skirt, say, you'll need to take in the lining too.

Question 121:
How can I take out some of the fullness in an elastic-waisted skirt?

There are two ways to take in the fullness of a skirt if the waist is gathered with elastic. The easiest way is to alter the skirt in the exact same way as you would alter an A-line skirt to be straighter. You would begin by taking the skirt in right underneath where the elastic is attached.

The other method, which will also be neater, is to remove the elastic and take out the fullness at the waist before putting the elastic back in. If the elastic fit around the waist before you take out the fullness, you may not need to shorten the elastic.

Rip out the stitches that hold the waistband to the skirt inside the waist. Open out the waistband. If the elastic is stitched down, unpick this stitching at the side seams for about 5cm (2in). Take in the skirt at the sides as required including the waistband, stitching the new seams and trimming away the excess fabric (see Question 119); you will have to lift the elastic out of the way to do this. Press the new seams open. If wished, you can restitch the elastic to the waistband. Fold the waistband back down and use a hemming stitch (see Question 40) to re-attach to the top of the skirt.

If you need to take in the elastic too, do this before you re-stitch the waistband in place. Fold the elastic and stitch across it to take in the amount required; trim the seam about 3mm (⅛in) from the stitching. Then stitch the elastic back down on the adjusted waistband.

ABOVE If the waistband is stitched down at top and bottom, you will need to rip out both lines of stitching before you can take out the elastic.

Question 122:
How do I determine what needs to be fixed or altered on trousers?

Try on the trousers and look at yourself in the mirror. If they are too long or too baggy it will be obvious straight away. If they are too baggy, work out where the excess is; they may be too baggy on your legs only and so not need adjusting round the hips. Are they too high in the waist? Turn round and try and look at your back view. Do the trousers gape at the back of the waist? (If your back curves inwards noticeably this is called a sway back.) Walk around in the trousers and then sit down. Do they feel uncomfortable? Are they too tight in the crotch seam?

Question 123:
What are my options?

There are many alterations that can be done to ready-made garments. However, several of these fixes are a little more involved than others and may need to be done by a professional. There are some problems that are usually unfixable; trousers that are too tight in the crotch are hard to remedy, although you can try the alteration in Question 124. Unfortunately, once the trousers are cut, fabric cannot be added. There are, thankfully, several alterations that can be done by a beginner: small adjustments to the crotch depth, rehemming trousers, waistband adjustments, and taking in at the legs.

Question 124:
How can I adjust the crotch depth?

If your trousers are too high and you want to make them lower without taking the whole waistband off, then you can shorten the crotch depth. This is done by simply stitching a deeper inner leg. Turn the trousers inside out. Start pinning the inner leg seam 12.5–15cm (5–6in) below the crotch intersection seam on one leg. Continue to the crotch seam, making the amount taken from the original seam greater as you get closer to the crotch seam until the width is 5mm (¼in). Repeat on the other leg. Tack the alteration in place and try the trousers on before stitching the new seam.

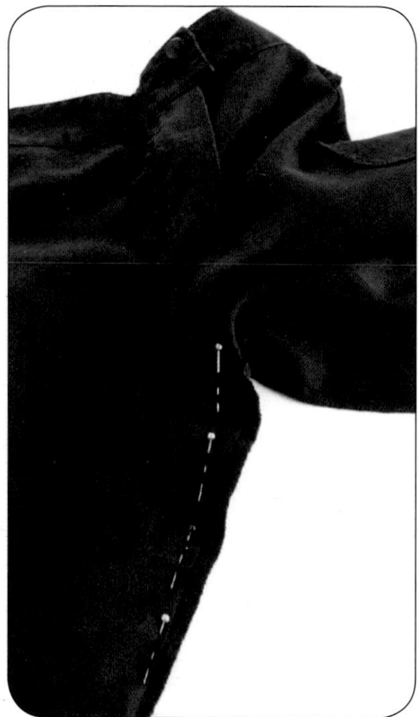

ABOVE To shorten the crotch depth, take in the inner leg seams. Pin and tack, then try on to check the fit before machine sewing in place.

It's harder to make more room in the crotch – once trousers are cut and sewn, there is not usually a way to make them larger in the crotch or rear end area. However, you can try to lower the crotch seam. Turn the trousers inside out. Pin the front crotch seam from where the crotch seam intersects the inner leg seam for about 7.5cm (3in) (or up to the end of the zip if there is one); make the new seam 5mm (¼in) wide to start and then taper to nothing. Repeat on the back crotch seam. Tack and then try the trousers on before stitching the new seam.

You won't be able to lower the crotch seam too much; if the trousers were originally at your waist and you lower them more than 1cm (½in) or so, they may not fit around your abdomen.

Question 125:
How can I take in trouser legs if they are too baggy?

This is quite a simple alteration and is very similar to taking in the side seams of a skirt. Turn the trousers inside out and try them on. Pin the side seams to the required amount; don't be surprised if you have to take in different amounts on either side – our legs and hips aren't always even!

Take the trousers off, taking care not to prick yourself with the pins. You may find it useful to mark the new seam line with tailor's chalk, since it isn't always easy to get the pins in a straight line. Stitch the new seams and then try on again to make sure the fit is right before trimming and finishing the seam.

EXPERT TIP

"You will need someone else's help to pin the side seams while trying on trousers; if you have to do this alteration on your own, start by pinning the side seams to what you think might be the right amount. Then try the trousers on – avoiding pricking yourself with pins. You may have to have a few goes at this before you get it right."

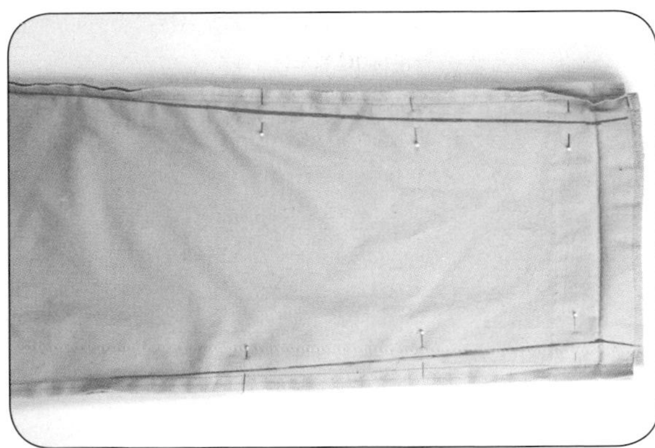

LEFT Use a marker to draw in the new seam and to give yourself a neat line to follow when stitching.

Question 126:
How can I turn long trousers into cropped ones?

Try on the trousers inside out and decide how much shorter you want them to be. Turn up the hems and pin the new turnings in place – you may need to get someone to help you with this. Take the trousers off and tack the new hem in place, stitching about 5mm (¼in) from the foldline. Remove the pins and press the new hem in place. Try on again to be sure the length is as you want it before you trim off any excess fabric from the hem. Make the new hem allowance about 5cm (2in) deep. Turn under the raw edge and pin. Hem (see Question 40) and then press to finish.

EXPERT TIP

“If you want the bottom of the shortened trousers to be narrower, take in the trouser legs first – as in Question 125.”

ABOVE After you've pinned up the hem the required amount, tack in place close to the foldline – this enables you to trim off the excess without unfolding the new hem.

Question 127:
How do I turn jeans into shorts?

First decide the length you want the shorts; put on the jeans and make a small mark where you think you'd like the fabric to end. Take off the jeans and mark all round each leg 5cm (2in) below the first mark. Cut the legs at the marked point. If you want hemmed edges, finish the cut edge of the fabric and then turn under and hem with catch stitch (see Question 41). If you want frayed edges, simply put the jeans in the washing machine and then dry in the dryer. The edges will fray and curl slightly. To get the amount of fraying you want, however, you may need to wash the shorts a few times. If the fraying continues in excess, you can sew a line of stitching around each leg above the beginning of the fraying.

Question 128:
How can I keep the faded-look hem on jeans, but still make them shorter?

If you want to take up a garment but wish to keep the original hemline, then there is a hem you can do. This type of hem is called a French hem (nothing to do with the French seam) or the European hem and is usually done on jeans or any garment with a unique hem (see Question 129). It can be used on other types of trousers, skirts, dresses and even sleeves.

With this type of hem you do need to use a sewing machine and once the French hem is cut and sewn, you cannot let it down again.

Question 129:
How do I do a French hem?

Before hemming the jeans you should first decide by how much you want to turn up the hem. Try on your jeans with the shoes that you will most likely be wearing with them. Fold up the hem to the outside of your jeans to the length that you like to wear them. Put a few pins in each leg to hold the hem in place and carefully take off your jeans. As with any hemming or altering, measure first, pin up and try on – a few times if needed. Doing this always takes less time than having to take out what you have just sewn. If you will be wearing heels with this specific pair of jeans, you might want the jeans a little longer. The jeans should fall 2.5–4cm (1–1½in) above the floor at your heel.

Pin all the way around the leg. Measure the hem you have just turned and then divide that number in half. For the purposes of this explanation, let's imagine the jeans need to be turned up 8cm (3in); 4cm (1½in) is, therefore, the measurement to use. The reason you cut the measurement in half is because you will be folding up the hem in half and actually hemming the full 8cm (3in).

Unpin the turned up hem and then adjust it until it measures 4cm (1½in) from the edge of the original hem to the fold; pin (see picture top right). Use a zip foot for your sewing machine if you have it – this allows you to stitch close to the original hem. If you don't have one, adjust the sewing-machine needle as far to the left as is possible. Make sure that you are using an appropriate foot – if you do not, the needle will come down on the foot itself and break. Stitch all the way around the leg bottom, stitching close to the edge of the original hem and being careful not to sew the leg opening together. Try the jeans on again to make sure you are happy with the length. Turn them right side out and tuck the hemmed area upwards. The stitching line around the new hem will form a seam on the right side directly above the original hem's stitching; it will be virtually invisible. Press the new hem flat (see bottom right).

To keep the French hem from showing you can trim and leave raw edge as is, ironing it up or down after each washing. Alternatively, use some fusible hemming tape and fuse the hem upwards on the inside.

ABOVE Work out by how much you need to shorten the jeans. Divide this by half. Turn up the jeans to this measurement and pin in place.

ABOVE The French hem will leave a barely visible seam just above the original hem stitching. Press this seam to give a neat finish.

Question 130:
What is a dart?

Darts are usually triangular tucks that are wide at one end and tapered at the other end. The most common dart is probably the one often seen at the bustline of women's blouses which helps the fabric fit closer to a woman's curves. Princess seams are also a type of dart, but they are much longer and often shape an entire dress bodice lengthwise. A dart may also be placed in the back of a shirt or blouse to take in fullness through the back or to shape the blouse to the shoulders.

Darts in trousers and skirts help to fit the garment closer to the waist. The darts are wide enough at the waistband to take up all the extra looseness in your waist, and then taper downward toward your hips, which need less dart and more fabric. The length of your darts will depend on the shape of your hips. If you have high, square hips your darts will taper sharply, whereas if you have a long gently sloping hip line, they will taper more gradually.

LEFT On a shirt patterned with diagonal stripes, the bust darts are clearly visible where the stripes cross over at the bust area.

Question 131:
How do I add a dart at the waist?

If the trousers or skirt and their waistband are a lightweight fabric, you can simply create a dart in the waistband. First try on the skirt and decide how much you want to take in; divide by two since you want to make two darts. Measure mid-way between the centre back and side seams. Fold the garment right sides together and pin the amount you wish to take in for each dart. Using a regular straight stitch, sew from the top of the waistband, down the skirt, ending the point one stitch away from the actual trousers or skirt back. As you approach the point of the dart, shorten the stitch length and sew off the end of the fabric. Leave a long tail of thread, before cutting the thread from the machine. Hand knot the thread at the end of the dart. Trim the threads. Repeat for the other dart.

For heavier weight skirts and trousers, you will still be creating a dart, however you need to separate the waistband and open it up – plus a few more centimetres – in the area you will be sewing the dart. You should separate the waistband from the skirt enough so that the waistband can be opened to lie flat. Take in the dart as before but into the opened-out waistband too.

Question 132:
How do I put darts in an elasticated waistband?

Usually, the elastic waistband is not the problem, it is the skirt itself that is too big. The easiest way to do this is to take a small dart in the waistband as shown in Question 131.

Open out the waistband as described in the second part of Question 131 and separate the elastic from the waistband (if it is stitched down). Make the darts as described and then re-attach the elastic to the skirt. If the elastic is now too long, shorten it before re-attaching (see Question 121).

Question 133:
How do I place elastic only in the back of the waistband?

Adding elastic to just the back of trousers can be a little bit easier than the entire waistband. First buy some elastic that is a little narrower than the waistband of the trousers. The narrower the elastic is, the more gathers will be created when the waistband is sewn back on. Then look and see if there are any belt loops on the back; they will need to be taken off.

Start by ripping out the stitches that hold the inside-back waistband to the waistline, including stitches about 2.5cm (1in) beyond the side seams. Cut a piece of elastic that fits comfortably from one side seam to the other on your back waistline. Mark the exact centre of the elastic. About 1cm (½in) from each end of the elastic, sew it to the side seam front (you are making the elastic 2.5cm (1in) shorter this way). You can also sew the exact centre of the elastic to the back seam by stitching-in-the-ditch on the outside. Since you have made the elastic shorter, you will need to stretch it a little. Turn the waistband back over the elastic. Try the trousers on and walk around and sit down to make sure that they are not too tight in the back. When you are happy with the fit, take the trousers off and use a hemming stitch to reattach the waistband at the waist.

EXPERT TIP

“Stitching in the ditch is when stitching follows an existing seam line. Most sewing machines have a special foot (sometimes called the edging foot or piping foot) that lets you follow the original seam (the ditch) exactly. Use a thread the same or slightly darker colour than the garment.”

Question 134:
How do I replace the old elastic in a waistband?

If the elastic in a garment perishes or breaks, the first thing you need to do is determine how the old elastic is sewn in. If the elastic is just attached in a few places, figure out where it is stitched down and rip out those stitches. Open up a seam in the waistband and pull out the old elastic. Cut a new piece as long as the old plus another 5cm (2in).

Use a safety pin to pin one end of the elastic to one side of the opened seam. Attach another safety pin to the other end of the elastic. Feed this safety pin and the elastic through the waistband starting at the slit that you opened. When you get all the way around, pull the end of the elastic out. Unattach the other end of the elastic from the first safety pin. Then either safety-pin or loosely knot the ends of the elastic together. Try the garment on and pull the elastic where it is pinned to the point where you want the elastic sewn. Mark that spot. Remember to walk around and sit down in the garment. Don't make the elastic too tight. When you're happy with the fit, trim the ends of the elastic to about 1cm (½in) and overlap the ends; tack together. Pin the elastic to the marked spot and zigzag stitch in place to the waistband. Tuck in the seam allowances where the seam was opened out and hand sew closed with small slip stitches.

If the elastic is attached to the waistband you will need to rip out the stitches holding the waistband to the inside of the skirt or trousers. Unfold the waistband and rip out the stitches holding the old elastic; discard. Cut your new elastic to the length required and then pin to the top part of the folded out waistband, pinning only at the seams. Make sure you are pinning the elastic to the part of the waistband that will not be seen on the right side. Stretch the elastic out and pin all round the waistband. Using a wide zigzag stitch or straight stitch, sew the garment and elastic together with a 3mm (⅛in) seam allowance, stretching the elastic in between the pins. Refold the waistband over the elastic and then use a hemming stitch to re-attach the edge of the waistband to the skirt or trousers.

135 How can I fix the gaps in the bust area of my ready-made blouses?

136 The neckline on my tank top is too low; can I fix this?

137 How can I make a top more custom fitted?

138 How do I use darts to alter tops?

139 How would I add front darts?

140 How would I add darts in the back of my garment?

141 What are princess seams?

142 How do I take in a dress or top at the sides?

143 How do I take in the back seam?

144 How can I add a pleat to the centre back?

145 My jacket is too tight; what can I do?

146 My jacket is too loose; what can I do?

147 How do I alter a lined jacket?

148 How do I shorten a sleeve?

149 How do I shorten lined sleeves?

150 How do I shorten cuffed sleeves?

151 How can I make sleeves narrower around the wrist?

152 How can I take in sleeves without stitching a new seam?

153 Can I use elastic to make sleeves narrower at the wrist?

154 How do I take up the shoulders on shoulder seams with set-in sleeves?

155 How can I attach a shoulder pad – both permanently and temporarily?

156 The neckline has stretched out on my favourite t-shirt; what can I do?

157 I've just had a baby and really like one of my maternity dresses; is it possible to take it in?

8

ALTERING TOPS, DRESSES AND JACKETS TO FIT

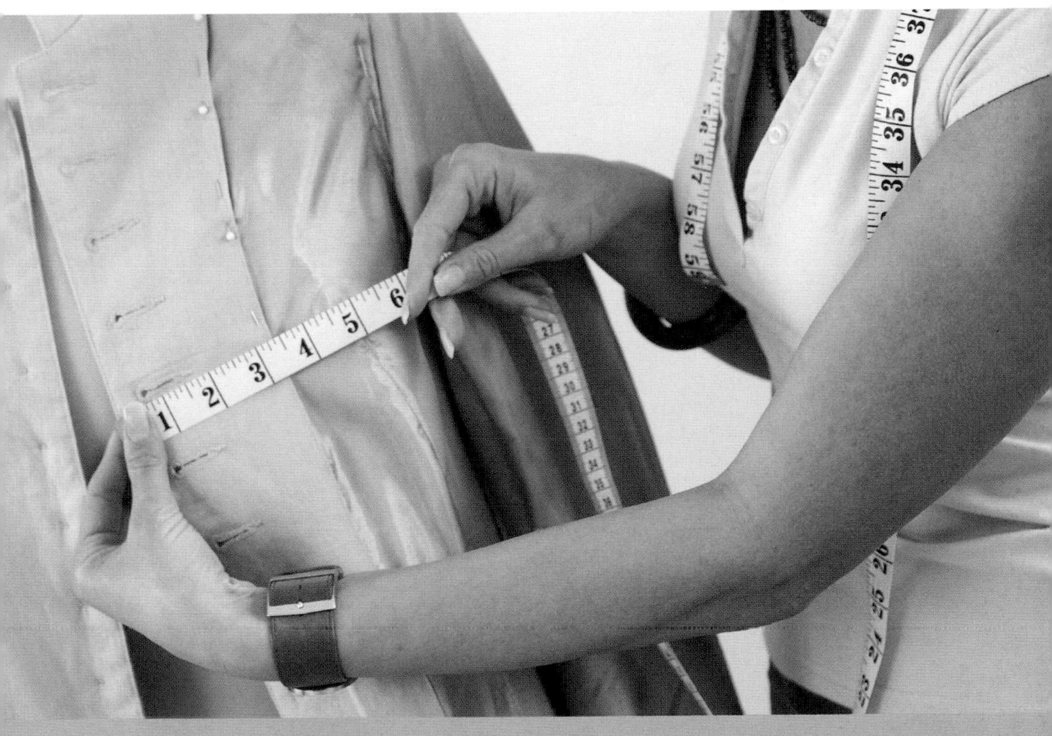

Question 135:
How can I fix the gaps in the bust area of my ready-made blouses?

If our bodies were all shaped the same, then clothes created to the standard measurements would fit us perfectly. Of course this is rarely the case! One of the places where fit can often be a problem is the bust area on women's button-front blouses. No matter where the buttons lie on the front opening, and unless the blouse is very loose, certain movements will cause the blouse to gap in this area. For larger busted women, this is a constant problem and one that probably has turned many of them away from buying button-front blouses. However, there is a fix you can do.

First, make sure that the blouse fits correctly everywhere else. This is not a solution to wearing clothes that are too small; this is a solution for blouses that look fine when you are standing still, but when you start to move around, the gap appears. Then all you need to do is sew a small press stud (see Question 55) in the area that gaps. Use more than one if you think it's necessary. If you are worried that the press stud will show – through a fine or sheer fabric, say – you can purchase clear plastic press studs.

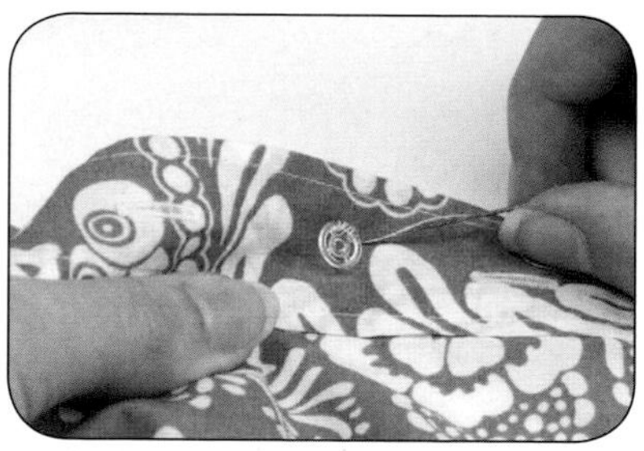

ABOVE Stitch clear plastic press studs to a blouse made of lightweight fabric.

EXPERT TIP

“If you want to make sure you sew the press stud on in the right place, first use some stick-on Velcro. Cut a tiny piece and place it on your blouse where you think the press stud should go. Button up the blouse and walk around. Is the Velcro in the right place? If not, move the Velcro pieces up and down. When everything is in the right place, remove the Velcro, place a pin in the spot, then sew the snap on.”

Question 136:
The neckline on my tank top is too low; can I fix this?

If you wear tank tops and shell tops and find the necklines are too low, you can fix this by taking them up at the shoulder. Fortunately, such tops have narrow shoulder seams, which make them even easier to alter.

Simply try on the tank top inside out and pull up on the shoulders until you have the front at the level you want. Usually this is only a small amount. Make sure that you do not pull up too far so that the armholes are too tight. Pin and then take the top off. Add a few more pins to hold, making sure that the straps are even. Using the correct needle for the fabric (most tank tops are knit) in the sewing machine, sew the amount you wish to take up.

After you have sewn the straps shorter, you have a few options for finishing the shoulder seams. If the fabric is very thin and the amount you have taken in is small, you can simply press the seam toward the back, where it will show less, and topstitch. If the seam is too bulky, trim to about 1cm (½in). Press the seam open. Topstitch the edges of each strap, sewing down the excess fabric. If you feel that the fabric will fray (knits should be fine), turn under the seam allowances, press, and topstitch.

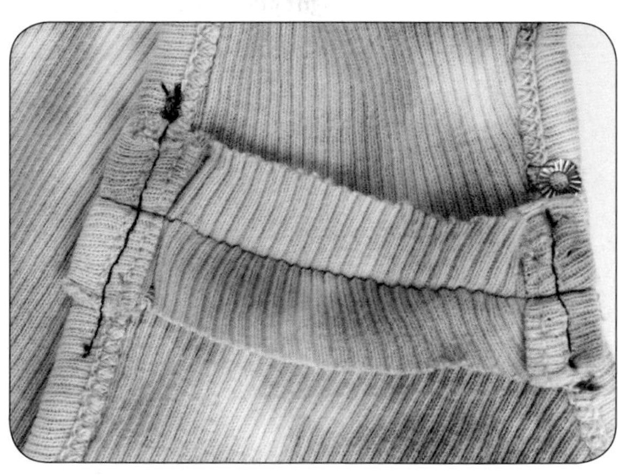

LEFT To reduce bulk in your new shoulder seam, open it out, press, and then topstitch down at the sides.

Question 137:
How can I make a top more custom fitted?

If you have a top that you love, but it's just too big in certain areas, there may be a few things that you can do to make it more fitted. First, put the top on and see if just taking in the side seams will help. The amount you take in should be a little more in the waist area. If this will not help or it helps, but is not enough, there are a few other alterations you can do.

First, check over the top – does it have darts, princess seams, a centre back seam? If you can, you want to work with whatever fitting seams the top currently has. You cannot take in a horizontal bust dart any futher than it is already unless the entire side of the blouse is taken apart, and the bodice back is also rehemmed, which is a major undertaking.

If the top does have vertical darts, begin by putting the blouse on inside out and pinning these darts in so they are a little tighter. Remember to do the same thing equally on both sides of the garment (unless you are very different on each side). Do one set of alterations at a time and try on the top after each to see if they work. Make sure you do not make the top too tight!

Question 138:
How do I use darts to alter tops?

As you learned in Question 130, darts are wedge-shaped tucks taken in various parts of garments to make them fit closer to the body. They are more often found in clothing for women. The most common dart is probably the horizontal one seen at the bustline of women's blouses, which helps the fabric fit closer over the curve of a woman's bust. Just as it would be hard to adjust an existing bust dart, so would it be difficult to add a new dart to a ready-made garment.

However, it's usually a simple matter to sew in vertical darts. These can be placed in the back of a shirt or blouse to take in fullness through the back or to shape the blouse to the shoulders or even the back of a skirt waistband.

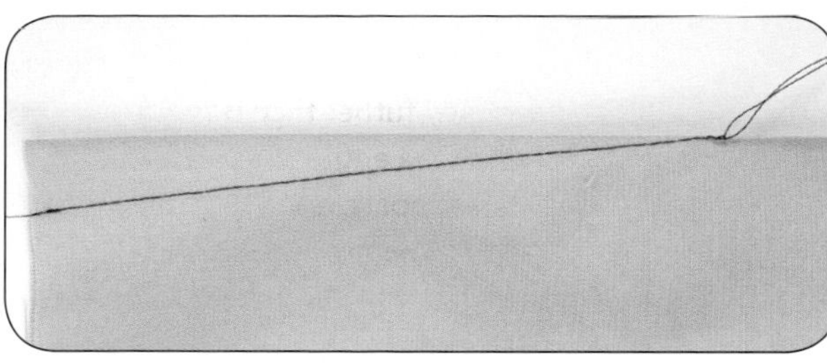

LEFT Darts can be wedge shaped; you start by taking in the required amount and then taper to a point.

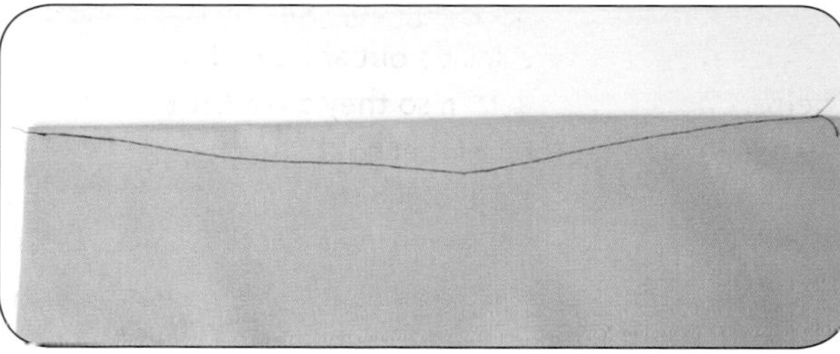

LEFT Darts can also start from nothing, widen to the amount you want to take in and then taper to nothing again.

Question 139:
How would I add front darts?

For this question and the next, the darts in question are vertical ones, and not horizontal bust darts. As seen above, there are two shapes for darts. A simple dart is wedge shaped; wide at one end and tapering to nothing at the point. Or a dart can be wide in the middle, tapering to points on either side.

A front dart should begin right under the bust area, starting from nothing, and then becoming wider at the waistline, before tapering back to nothing before it reaches the hip area; another wider area where you will want the fabric to lie flat. If you are going to sew a dart all the way to the bottom of a blouse, do not take the dart to the edge. Leave the dart about 2.5cm (1in) wide at the blouse edge, otherwise the blouse will not lie properly.

Question 140:
How would I add darts in the back of my garment?

Adding back darts can be done in exactly the same way as adding front darts. Either take the top or jacket off, pin in the darts, and try on a few times, until you've got it right. Or have someone else pin the garment for you, while you wear it inside out. Make sure that you lift your arms and move about – you always need plenty of room in the back of garments. You may want to make the dart pointed at both ends. You might want it extending to the edge of the blouse or only to the waistline.

If you sew right up to the shoulder seams – either in the back or front – this is still considered a dart, but is called a princess seam (see Question 141).

Remember, that what you take in on the left side, you must take in the same amount on the right side. Do not take in one dart on one side by so much that there is not enough excess left for two. Press darts toward the centre seam; front darts are pressed toward the centre front, back darts toward the centre back. Remember to use a pressing cloth.

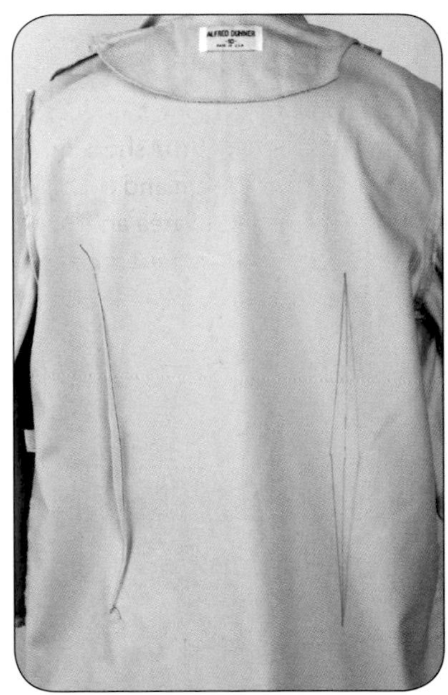

ABOVE When you've pinned in your back dart it's a good idea to use a marker to draw in its position. It's easier to stitch straight along a drawn line than a line of pins.

Question 141:
What are princess seams?

Princess seams are a type of dart, but they are much longer and may even fit an entire dress bodice lengthwise. They are almost like two dart wedges placed larger sides together. Princess seams get wider where the body is narrower, specifically at the waist. For example, on a top front, a princess seam would begin at the shoulder seam or armhole seam and continue over or near the bust area and down to the hemline, tapering to absolutely nothing. Princess seams usually go directly down to the hemline of the garment, however if you are adding one to a ready-made garment, then the point should end about 2.5cm (1in) before the hem edge of the garment. This will let the garment lie smoothly. In the bodice back, a princess seam can begin at the shoulder seam and continue down over the shoulder blades, widening at the waist and narrowing as it tapers toward the garment hemline.

LEFT Princess seams start at the shoulder, then run down the body, curving over the bust, to the hem.

Question 142:
How do I take in a dress or top at the sides?

First try on the dress or top inside out and pin the side seams until you've taken in the required amount. You will need help with this; if you have to do it on your own, pin the seams first and then try the dress on.

Start pinning at the top of the seam, at the armhole; start from nothing and then gradually widen how much you are taking in. You may want to take in more at the waist than the hips. If you want the dress or top to retain the original width at the hem, gradually taper the seam to nothing at this point. If you want to reduce the width of the garment at the hem too, make the new seam take a bit in here as well. Make sure that the dress or top still lies smoothly in the back and front areas; if you take in too much, you will create unattractive pull lines, which makes the garment look ill-fitted and tight.

If the dress is sleeveless, you could take in the seams under the arm too, to make sure the armholes don't gape. Make sure the seams on either side are equal and match at the key points (bust, waist and hip); if the side seams are uneven, the dress or top won't hang straight. Once you are happy with the new shape of the garment, stitch the new seams in place. Try it on again, to be extra sure of the fit. Trim off any excess fabric and then finish the raw edges of the seams; this is important because side seams get a lot of wear and will fray quickly if you don't finish the edges. Press the seams open.

Question 143:
How do I take in the back seam?

This is just as simple as taking in the side seams. According to how much you wish to take in from the back seam, there are a few ways to do this alteration. On bespoke men's suits, this is where most alterations begin. The suit is fitted and altered before the collar is sewn on.

Once again, try on the top inside out and pin or have someone pin the back. Usually you will want to take it a little more at the waist area. Sew a dart, beginning in a point, taking in more at the waist area and ending in a point. Try on the top right side out. For this dart, you need to be careful that you do not take in too much – otherwise the back hemline of the top will not lie smoothly.

A more complicated way to take in the back seam is to separate the facing or trim at the top back seam, take in the back seam as well as the facing or trim and sew them back together again. If the top has a collar, this becomes a much more complicated alteration and is probably best done by a tailor.

ABOVE To take in the back seam, begin pinning at the top of the original seam, and then widen the amount taken in as you go down the seam.

Question 144:
How can I add a pleat to the centre back?

To help fit a top that is too big, especially in the back, you can try to add a pleat to the back to take out some of the fullness. This will only work with very loose tops that you want to be a just little more fitted; it cannot work if you want the top completely fitted because the pleat will only hang correctly on a loose top.

About half way between the centre back and side seams and in the waist area (this doesn't need to be exact, but does need to be the same on both sides of the centre back) pinch out about 1cm (½in) on either side to start with and pull to the centre back. Pin and do the same with the other side. Try the top on and see how it feels. Once you have adjusted the pleat the way you want you can stitch the pleat down from the inside or stitch on some buttons for decoration to help hold it down.

Question 145:
My jacket is too tight; what can I do?

I bought the nicest suit jacket for work in a second-hand clothing shop recently. I had tried it on and checked the back for fit, buttoned it, it felt like it fitted and it was a good deal. When I got home, I realised that it was actually a double-breasted jacket; in other words it had two rows of vertical buttons at the opening. So when I buttoned up the jacket with the second set of buttons, it turned out to be quite tight. To fix the fit, I simply took off the second set of parallel buttons.

If I had wanted to keep the jacket double breasted, or if it had been a tight single-breasted jacket, then another fix would have been to move the buttons. To do this, simply decide on how much looser you want your jacket and then move the buttons that distance in, towards the jacket opening. Mark the new position of the buttons with crossed pins or tailor's chalk, and unpick the stitching that holds the button in place with care. Then simply stitch the buttons in their new positions.

EXPERT TIP

“ When you remove the buttons from their old position you may have holes or an indentation left on the fabric. If the fabric of your jacket can be ironed, try pressing them out first; use steam (if possible) and a pressing cloth. If that doesn't work, or if the garment can't be ironed, try hanging the jacket up in a steamy bathroom and then gently tease the fibres into place with a fingertip. Failing that, take the jacket to the cleaners and see if there is anything they can do. ”

ABOVE To add more room in a jacket, you can simply move the buttons in towards the opening.

Question 146:
My jacket is too loose; what can I do?

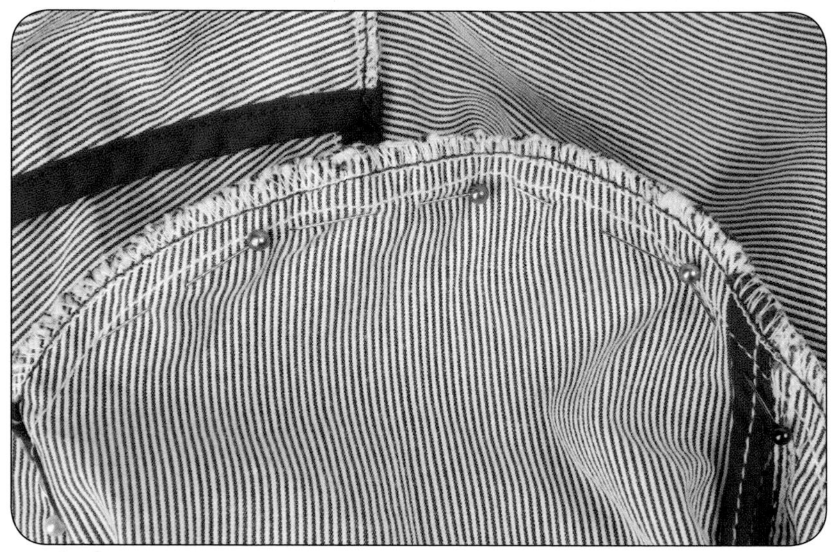

ABOVE To reduce bagginess in the shoulders, take in the seam at the armhole very slightly. Pin the new seam in and try on the jacket inside out to check the fit.

As mentioned in Question 145, if the jacket has a front closure, you can move the buttons, press studs or even hooks over a little. Mark exactly where you want to them to be. Carefully, take the old buttons off, but leave the thread so that you can make sure that you are aligning the closure at the same level, just more to the right or left.

You can also do a little pinning to see if the jacket fits better by taking in the sides or maybe some front or back darts or try taking in the back seam or a combination of all. Remember jackets are usually designed to be worn over a top, no matter how lightweight, so you want to make sure that the jacket is not made too tight.

If you've taken the jacket in at the front (by moving buttons) or at the side seams, it may remain a little baggy at the shoulders. You can take in the seam between the sleeve and the armhole opening, but only by a very small amount. Take in too much and the angle of the sleeve will alter and the jacket will not hang as well.

Try on the jacket inside out and pin around the armhole; start at the top and then taper to nothing a few centimetres from the point where the armhole seam and side seam meet. Take in no more than 5mm (¼in) at the top. Try the jacket on again and make sure that the alteration hasn't changed the sleeve fit too much. Stitch the seam in place. Since you are only taking in a small amount, you can probably leave the new seam as it is. But if it's a lightweight jacket you may want to trim the new seam slightly; remember to finish raw edges.

Question 147:
How do I alter a lined jacket?

If the jacket is lined and the lining is attached to the jacket, you will need to separate the lining if you want to take in the sides or back seams or create darts.

Ideally, try to separate the jacket from the lining in only one place for all of these alterations. If the jacket has a back seam, start there. Rip out the seam for a centimetre and try to turn the jacket inside out. If the ripped-out seam is not large enough, rip out a little bit more but be very careful that you do not actually tear the seam or put holes in the lining. If the jacket lining does not have a back seam, separate the jacket at the bottom edge where the lining meets the garment fabric at the hem. Again, take out only a few inches and try to turn the jacket inside out here. You need only to separate the jacket from the lining in one place for all of these alterations. When you are done, turn the jacket back right side out, press and slip stitch closed where you had separated the jacket from the lining.

Question 148:
How do I shorten a sleeve?

If you are shortening sleeves that are finished at the wrist with just a hem, then the answer is to turn under a new hem. Try the garment on and turn up a new hem on each sleeve; pin in place. Take the garment off and turn inside out. Tack the new hem in place, about 1cm (½in) from the fold. Take out the pins, turn to the right side and try on again to make sure you are happy with the length. Take it off and turn to the wrong side again. If necessary, trim the excess fabric from the new hem and turn under the raw edge. Press and hem (see Question 40).

You can also take a tuck in a sleeve. Do this part way down the sleeve – ideal if the sleeve is made in two parts and already has a seam – or at the cuff. The technique is the same as used to make a French hem in jeans (see Question 129).

Question 149:
How do I shorten lined sleeves?

Shortening lined sleeves can be a little more complicated, but it's still possible for the beginner. You will first need to understand how the sleeve is sewn together. On a lightweight jacket with lining, you may be able to separate the lining, then hem both the sleeve and the lining before sewing back together. However, on a more standard suit jacket, you may also have to deal with interfacing. The interfacing is usually placed about 2.5cm (1in) below the hem fold on the sleeve fabric that will eventually be turned up to the inside of the jacket. It then continues for 5–7.5cm (2–3in) above the hem fold on the actual sleeve. The hem of a jacket lies much smoother with interfacing.

If there is interfacing in the sleeve, you can take it out and not replace it; leave it as it is; or replace with new interfacing. Shortening the sleeve by 2.5–5cm (1–2in) should not matter as long as there is still interfacing on the hem fold and up through the sleeve fabric.

First, take off any cuff buttons that may get in the way. You can sew them back on afterward. Put the jacket on and measure and pin the sleeve where you would like the new hem line – you may need some help with this. Take the jacket off and turn the arms inside out. At the arm hem line, carefully separate the jacket fabric from the lining.

To replace the interfacing, simply take out the old interfacing (fusible interfacing can be peeled off) and cut a new piece of fusible that will go the width of the jacket sleeve from the bottom of the arm's length and about 10cm (4in) deep. Press in place according to the manufacturer's directions. Then continue with the hemming process of the sleeve.

Fold a new hem line inward at the same line that you pinned. Once the outer fabric is folded, fold the lining inward, so all the excess fabric is in between the jacket and the lining. The lining's hem should be folded up 1–2.5cm (½–1in) shorter than the jacket fabric so it does not stick out at the bottom of the jacket sleeve.

Make sure the folded hem is lying smoothly. Pin the lining to the jacket to keep in place. Press the hem to make a permanent crease. Then use catch stitch (see Question 41) to stitch the lining to the sleeve hem. Press and turn to the right side.

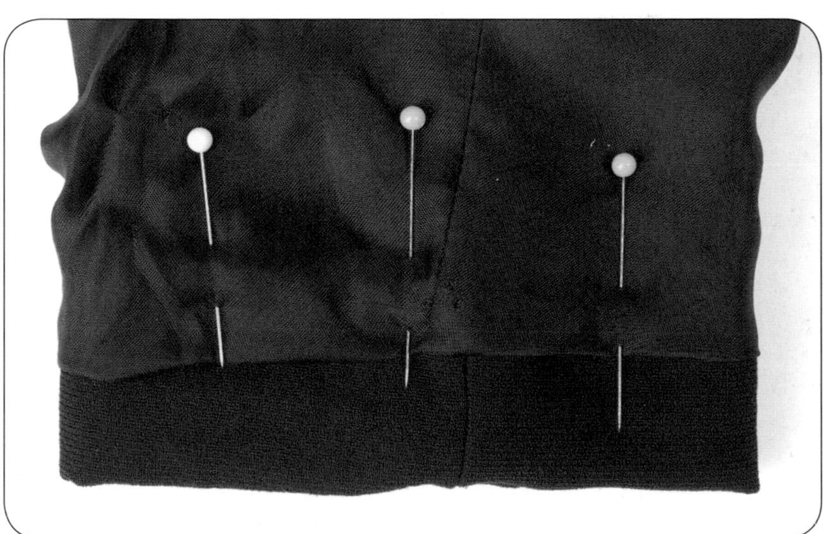

ABOVE Once you've turned up the new hem on the jacket, turn up and pin the lining in place. It should fall about 2.5cm (1in) above the edge of the sleeve.

Question 150:
How do I shorten cuffed sleeves?

Shortening a cuffed sleeve is also a little bit more complicated but achievable. However you choose to do it, the vent opening will become shorter. You will be shortening the actual sleeve, not the cuff itself.

The quick and easy way is to take a tuck, as you would for the French hem on jeans (see Question 129). The tuck should be located exactly where the cuff is sewn to the blouse.

The other, more professional way, is to remove the cuff and alter the sleeve before re-attaching the cuff. Look at the cuff to see how it is made and sewn to the shirt sleeve; it is formed of two pieces of fabric sewn wrong sides together and the actual sleeve is wedged inside and topstitched. Before you remove the cuff, there are a few things to mark or pin in place. Look at the sleeve and note any pleats in the fabric that help ease the fullness of the sleeve into the cuff. You want to retain these, so pin them in place and then tack once the cuff is removed. When you've shortened the sleeve you may have to make an additional pleat or gather in the fabric before reattaching the cuff.

You also need to mark the exact point where the cuff meets the side seam. And if you take off both cuffs at the same time, ensure you make a note of which cuff is right and which is left. If you sew the wrong cuff back on the wrong sleeve, it will be hard to button up.

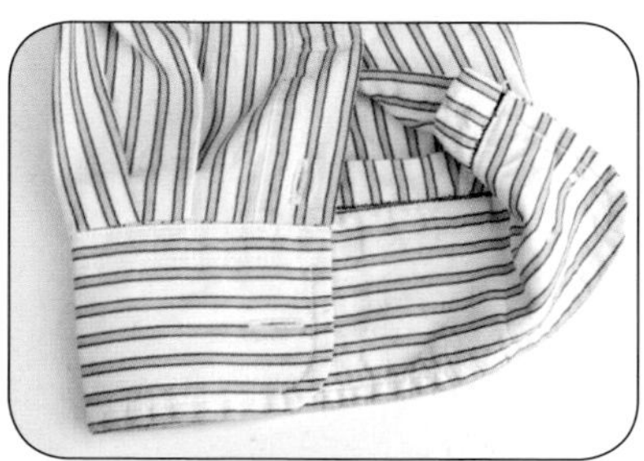

ABOVE The simplest way to shorten cuffed sleeves is to take a tuck in, just above the cuff, just as you would if you were doing a French hem.

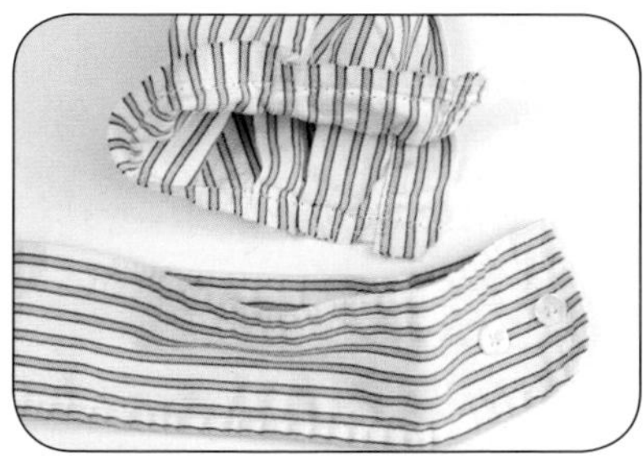

ABOVE You can also remove the cuff, cut off the excess length in the sleeve, and then re-attach the cuff. You may have to gather up any fullness.

A tailor would probably remove the placket and cut the vent opening longer and then resew the placket on. However, if the vent opening is long enough – even after shortening the sleeve and vent area – then you will be fine and do not need to remove, cut and re-apply the placket.

Using a seam ripper, carefully unpick the stitching that joins the cuff to the sleeve and separate the two parts. Cut off the amount of fabric from the sleeve that you want shortened, remembering to leave a 1.5cm ($^5/_8$in) allowance for the seam. Pin the cuff back on, slipping the shirt sleeve in between the two layers of the cuff; you will need to pleat or gather up the excess fabric slightly to fit. Tack and then machine stitch in place. Try to stitch along the line of the previous stitching as much as possible.

Question 151: How can I make sleeves narrower around the wrist?

There are several ways to do this, the first of which involves taking down the hem and decreasing the width of the sleeve at the wrist area, before rehemming. This is the best bet for knit fabrics that will stretch. For other options, see Questions 152 and 153.

First, turn the garment inside out and rip out the original hem of the sleeve. If you want to shorten the sleeve at the same time, trim off the excess fabric now, but remember to leave about 2.5cm (1in) longer for the hem turning.

Then pin a new seam into the sleeve. Take it in at the wrist by the amount you want to reduce the width and then pin along the old seam to either the elbow or underarm, tapering the new seam to nothing at this point. Try the garment on, making sure you can still get your hand out of the wrist. When you are happy with the reduction on both sleeves, stitch the new seam in place. Cut off the excess fabric, finish the raw edges and press the seam to one side. Turn up the hem again and restitch.

Question 152:
How can I take in sleeves without stitching a new seam?

You can narrow a sleeve by taking a pleat at the wrist and securing this with a button. To start, first decide how much narrower you want the sleeve. At the bottom edge of the sleeve, fold in a pleat and pin in place. Try the garment on to make sure you can get your hand through the opening and that the wrist is not too tight.

Take the top off and make sure the pleat you have made is neat and even before pressing into place. Stitch a button to one pressed edge of the pleat. Then make a thread loop (see Question 61) on the opposite pressed edge that fits over the button. You can then fasten the button to tighten the wrist, and then undo it to make taking the garment off easier.

If you prefer, you can simply stitch the pleat in place. Sew a button over the stitches to conceal them neatly.

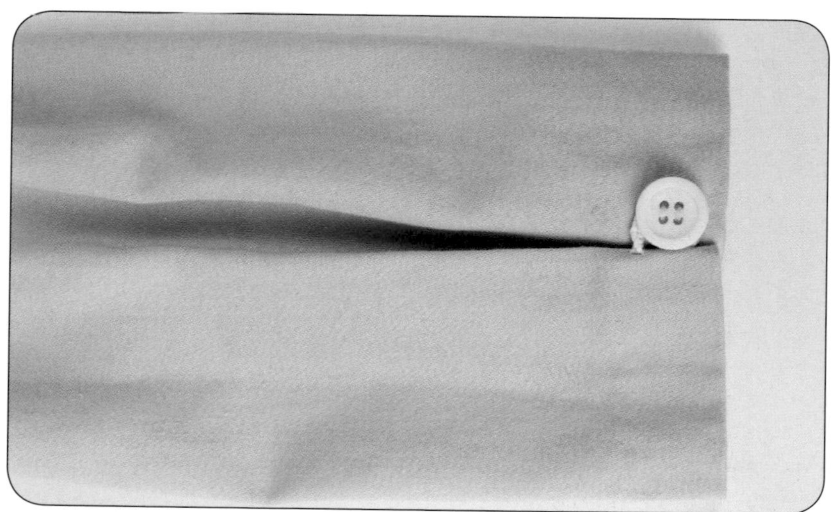

ABOVE You can reduce the width at the wrist by taking a pleat in the sleeve and then creating a button fastening.

Question 153:
Can I use elastic to make sleeves narrower at the wrist?

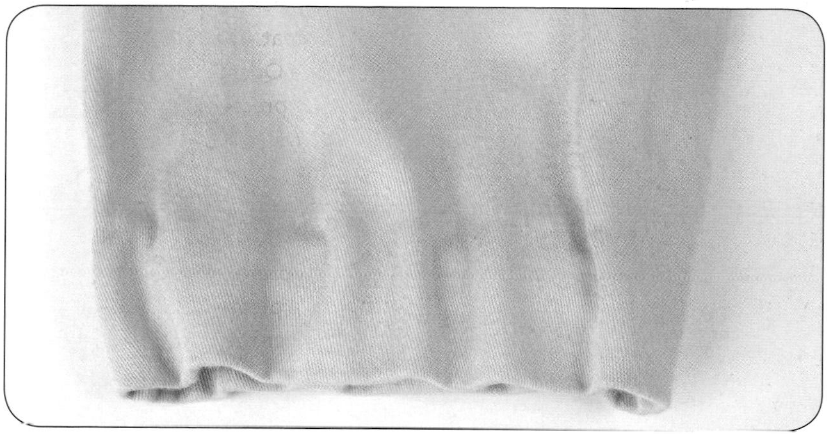

ABOVE If the sleeves of your jacket or top are hemmed at the wrist, then it's fairly simple to add some elastic which will draw in the fabric.

Try on the shirt or jacket and figure out if the sleeves need to be shortened as well as narrowed. It's best to do both jobs together.

If the shirt does not need to be shortened, you can open up the side seam inside the hem and slip some elastic in. Measure your wrist plus 2.5cm (1in). Cut the elastic to this length. Attach a safety pin to each end of the elastic. Pin one safety pin to the fabric at the opened seam to hold the elastic in place. Push the other safety pin into the opened seam and use to thread the elastic around the wrist hem. Continue as in Question 134 for replacing elastic in a skirt waistband.

If the sleeve needs to be hemmed; then measure, subtract an inch from the amount that you cut off, and cut if necessary. Fold up 1cm (½in), fold up again and hem, leaving a gap of about 2.5cm (1in). Thread the elastic through this gap and then slip stitch closed to finish.

Question 154:
How do I take up the shoulders on shoulder seams with set-in sleeves?

There are few ways to do this. The best way is a bit complicated and really needs to be done by a tailor, who will remove the entire sleeve and reshape the armhole and sleeve head (top of the arm). However, you can take up the shoulder seam by making the armhole seam allowance wider where the armhole meets the shoulder. This can only be done for about 1cm (½in) at the most without distorting the shoulder.

Mark about 5cm (2in) to the back and 5cm (2in) to the front from where the shoulder seam meets the armhole seam. As you sew, make the widest part at the shoulder seam. Make sure that your seam is smooth with no extra fabric or little gathers in the new seam.

You can also take a dart at the shoulder seam from the back to the front to pull the sleeve higher on the shoulder. This all depends on the fabric and pattern. You want to make sure that the darts which would not normally be in a shoulder seam will blend in.

If the fabric is lightweight, the dart can be in one long seam from the front over the shoulder seam to the back. But if the fabric is medium to heavy weight, it is best to take out the shoulder seam for about 2.5cm (1in). Sew a dart from the front shoulder seam and then another one from the back shoulder seam in the same place. Then sew the shoulder seam together matching the ends of the darts.

For a top with set-in sleeves, do not do this alteration for more than 1cm (½in) or so on each side, otherwise it will affect the area underneath the arm. But sometimes 1cm (½in) can make all the difference to the fit. Press (with a pressing cloth) very well.

Question 155:
How can I attach a shoulder pad – both permanently and temporarily?

Attaching shoulder pads is easy. You can either sew them in permanently or attach temporarily with some Velcro. A shoulder pad in a tailored jacket should extend from the armhole seam line about 1cm (½in), give or take. This ensures the jacket sleeve does not just drop down from the shoulder armhole seam and adds shaping to the shoulder.

Wearing the jacket, pin the shoulder pad in, moving it to the back and front to see where it looks and feels best; for example, if your shoulders slope forward a bit, moving the shoulder pad toward the back will help clothes lie more smoothly. Take the jacket off. Pin the shoulder pad in with more pins. Most times, the centre of the top of the shoulder pad would be attached to the shoulder seam, however if you have positioned the pad further back or forward, then sew it in the way it fits and looks best. Take the jacket off and stitch the pad to the shoulder seam of the garment. Then stitch it to the edges of the armhole seam.

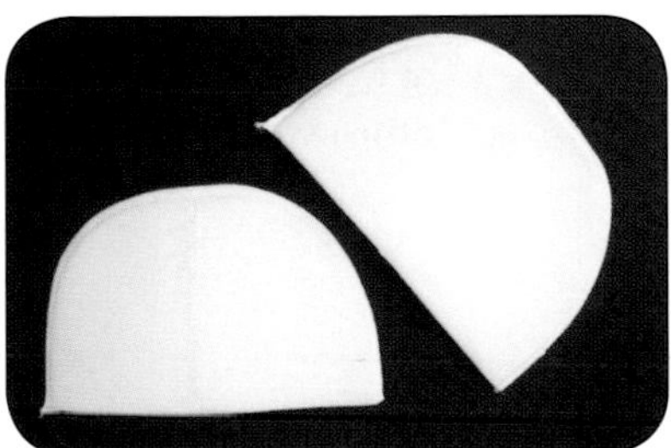

ABOVE Shoulder pads come in all shapes and sizes.

To attach shoulder pads temporarily, simply add Velcro to the shoulder padding and to the shoulder seams of those garments you want to add the pads to; this way, you can use just one pair of shoulder pads in several different garments. All you need to do is mark the position of the shoulder pad as for a permanent placing, and then stitch Velcro in the places where you would have had stitching. Remember to sew the hook side of the Velcro to the shoulder pad; you don't want the rougher part of the Velcro inside your jacket when the shoulder pad is not in place. Sew the loop side to your garment. Stitch other loop-side pieces of Velcro into all those other garments you want padded.

Question 156:
The neckline has stretched out on my favourite T-shirt; what can I do?

There are a few options you can try to fix a neckline that has stretched too much on a T-shirt or other cotton jersey garment. First try wetting the T-shirt and placing it in a hot dryer to see if the neck shrinks back to normal size (make sure that the T-shirt is machine washable and dryable first). Alternatively, dampen just the neckline area and then, with your iron on the highest setting, press the steam button while holding the iron close to, but not touching the T-shirt. (Only touch the iron to the T-shirt if you are sure it will not scorch.) With your hands, scrunch up the neckline a few inches at a time and continue steaming (watch that you do not burn your hands with the shots of steam). Let the T-shirt dry before you hang it up.

You could also try taking in small darts where the shoulder seam and neckline meet. This is fine for about 2.5cm (1in) or less on each side. This means losing up to 5cm (4in) on each shoulder seam, and 10cm (8in) around the entire neckline.

If the T-shirt is stretched out more than that, then try elastic. If the neckline hem is wide enough (more than 5mm (¼in)) use 5mm (¼in) elastic. Open the hem up for about 2.5cm (1in), and then use a safety pin to thread the elastic around the neckline. Make the neckline as tight as you want as long as the T-shirt lies flat and does not bunch up.

Question 157:
I've just had a baby and really like one of my maternity dresses; is it possible to take it in?

In most cases, there are always ways that you can alter a top to be smaller or more fitted, but it does depend on the style. Maternity clothes have more fabric in the front for obvious reasons. First take in the side seams, taking more in at the waist area. Since there is more fabric in the front of the top, when you take in the sides, the hem may be uneven and needs to be redone.

You can also create a tie back to take in some of the extra fabric. This works well with lightweight fabrics and summery styles. Take two pieces of ribbon, each about 45cm (18in) long, and pin them to the side seams at the waist. Try the dress on and tie the ribbons at the back. If the fit doesn't look quite right, move the position of the ribbons – they may work better pinned at a higher position, maybe just below the bust. When you are happy with the result, stitch the ribbons securely in place at the side seams. Check your hemline to see if it needs altering.

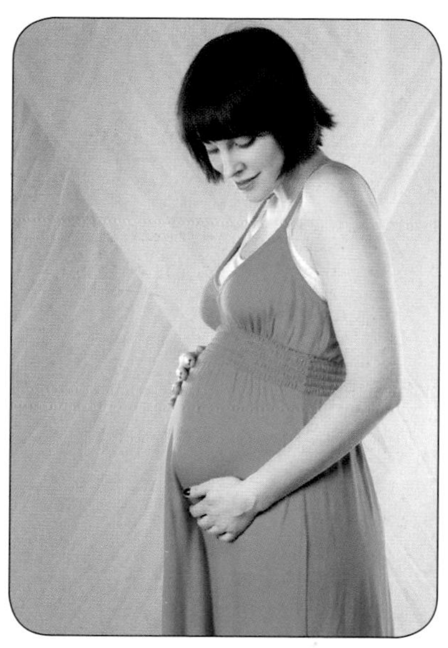

ABOVE Try adding a tie back to take in a summery maternity dress.

EXPERT TIP

“ Depending on how much weight you've lost after having your baby, you may find that simply belting your maternity dress creates a new look. ”

158 How do I give an old coat or jacket a new life?

159 How can I transform a dress into a tunic-style top?

160 How can I create a matching belt for a garment I have hemmed or made shorter?

161 How can I add belt loops to a garment?

162 How do I make covered buttons?

163 I don't like the curved hemlines on shirts that are worn over trousers; can this be altered?

164 T-shirts and knit tops are always too long for me; how can I shorten them?

165 How do I add a patch-style pocket to a garment?

166 How do I keep my straight-leg trousers tucked into my boots?

167 How can I make these straps for all of my straight-leg trousers?

168 What are kimono and dolman sleeves?

169 Is there any way to alter fuller-style sleeves?

170 How do I add a hood to a sweatshirt, jacket or coat?

171 Can I make the hood detachable?

172 Can I transform a long-sleeve T-shirt or sweatshirt into a cardigan?

9

ALTERING THE STYLE OF CLOTHING

Question 158:
How do I give an old coat or jacket a new life?

Probably the simplest solution is to change the buttons. There is a huge range of different and exciting buttons to be found. You can also source buttons that really go with the design of a garment; brass buttons for military-styled double-breasted coats, or leather buttons for tweedy jackets. You could also consider using covered buttons – see Question 162.

Another alternative is to change the collar or cuffs. This is a good option if your coat or jacket is frayed or worn in these areas. You can use a fleece fabric or even a fake fur to create a new winter look. Or try a contrasting colour or patterned fabric on a lightweight summer jacket.

You can also add a trim to the hemline or wrist. Look for interesting ribbons, lace or ric-rac to introduce colour and a new design element to the garment.

ABOVE Change a plain button to a more suitable leather one on a tweed jacket.

EXPERT TIP

“Once you have started a buttons stash, the buttons seem to multiply. Sometimes, I'll buy something at a flea market or in a charity shop just for the buttons. Many times at car boot sales, people are selling items that are ripped or stained, but still have beautiful buttons, like the old glass buttons from the past. It never hurts to check out these items since you never know when buttons from your stash will come in handy!”

Question 159:

How can I transform a dress into a tunic-style top?

It's quite straightforward to cut and hem a dress to transform it into a tunic-style top to wear with opaque tights, leggings or jeans. First put on the dress and decide what length you want the tunic to be. Will you be wearing a belt with it? If the answer is yes, then put the belt on now. Fold up a hem to the inside all round and pin in place. Look in the mirror and check that you like this length. If you don't have anyone to help you, pin up the hem before putting the dress on, then try it on to check the length. It's useful to have someone else's help when doing this first pinning as you will also want to check that the hem is even and level all round; the best way to do this is to get your helper to measure up from the floor to the foldline of the new hem.

Once you're happy with the amount you're taking up, take the dress off and place pins all along the fold of the newly pinned-up hem to mark the position of the foldline. Remove the pins that held the hem in place. Now measure down 5cm (2in); this will be your cutting line for the new hem. If you will be cutting off several inches from the dress, try to do it in one piece and you may be able to use this extra fabric as a matching scarf or belt for your new tunic (see Question 160). Once you have trimmed off the excess fabric, turn under and pin the raw edge (or finish with zigzag stitch). Then turn up the hem again and pin. Press and then hem.

If the tunic is a sweater knit or looser knit, you need only a 2.5cm (1in) deep hem. If you are sewing the hem on the sewing machine, make sure that you do not stretch out the fabric when sewing. You need to gently feed the garment through the sewing machine rather than pull or push it through.

Question 160:
How can I create a matching belt for a garment I have hemmed or made shorter?

As mentioned in Question 159, if the amount that you are cutting off the dress to create a tunic is quite deep, you can make a belt from this excess fabric.

You will also need some medium-weight iron-on interfacing. Take the piece of fabric that you have cut off your dress and if it is still in a circle, open up one side seam so you have one long piece. Fold the fabric in half lengthways, wrong sides together, and press. Measure the width of your strip and deduct 1.5cm (5⁄8in) for a seam allowance; measure the length of your strip and deduct 3cm (1¼in) for allowances. Cut a strip of interfacing this size. Open out the fabric and iron the interfacing along one lengthways half so it lines up with the fold. Fold the fabric right sides together, again lengthways, and stitch round the raw edges, leaving about 5cm (2in) open in one long side. Trim the seam and the corners. Turn the belt right side out through the 5cm (2in) gap. Slipstitch the opening closed; press. Add a buckle or use press studs to secure the belt during wear.

You can also make a belt from two strips of fabric sewn together, rather than a folded strip. Just remember to allow for 1.5cm (5⁄8in) seam allowances all round.

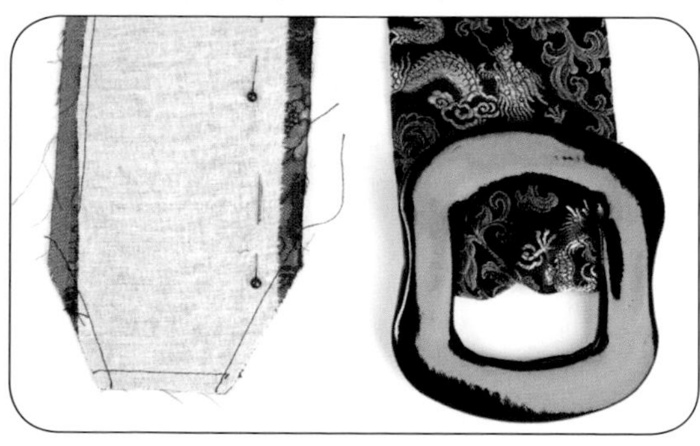

LEFT Cut two strips of fabric, or fold one strip in half lengthways, and iron on some interfacing before stitching round the edges.

Question 161:
How can I add belt loops to a garment?

If you wish to add belt loops to a garment, then you need to make thread chains and attach to the relevant places on your garment. Thread-chain belt loops are best added at the seams (side and back). Use a strong thread to make these belt loops – topstitching or embroidery thread are both ideal.

Find out the width of the belt you would want to wear with this garment; you will make the thread-chain belt loop about 2.5cm (1in) longer. Thread an embroidery needle (or a needle with a large enough eye to be able to pull the thicker thread through). Knot the thread with double thread.

If the dress does not have side seams, it would be advisable to begin and end the chain stitch belt loop in the exact same spot (not the exact same hole), instead of a few inches away. Insert the needle from the inside of the garment to the outside, pulling the needle through exactly where you want the belt loop to begin. Then insert the needle back into the fabric, close to where the thread emerges. Pull the thread through to the wrong side but not completely; leave a small loop on the right side. Bring the needle out again on the right side. Hold the loop open with the fingers on one hand, then use the other hand to pass the working thread (that still has the needle on it) through the loop. Pull a loop of the working thread through the first loop, then pull on this to tighten the first loop. Continue until you reach the length you decided you want for this garment, then add another inch. With the last loop, pull the working thread all the way through and pull to finish the chain. Take the thread end through to the inside of the garment, being careful not to pull the thread chain itself through to the inside of the garment. Knot the thread with a few knots so the chain stitch belt loop does not pull through. Cut the remaining thread.

Question 162:
How do I make covered buttons?

Covered buttons used to be the preserve of very upscale couture clothing, making everything match or coordinate on a garment; now anyone can make a matching covered button. You can buy an easy-to-use kit or you can cover a button you won't be using.

Buy a covered button kit in a craft or sewing store of the size you want the buttons. There are different types of kits available but the simplest to use features a metal button form with a serrated edge – which helps grasp the fabric – that you finish with a metal backing section. There is an aperture in this section, through which the shank on the button form protrudes.

Using the template provided with the kit, cut out a circle of fabric. Without knotting the thread and leaving a long piece of thread loose at the start, take some smallish stitches all round the edge of the fabric. They don't have to be perfect stitches – they won't be seen – but you do need to make several around the fabric circle, so they do have to be small enough for that. Make sure they are fairly close to the raw edge. Don't fasten off, and leave the thread loose at the end.

Place the button form to be covered face down on the wrong side of the fabric circle. Carefully pull on both ends of the loose thread to pull up the stitches and gather up the fabric. Tie the thread ends in a knot to secure. Tuck the raw edges of the material into the button form; the serrated edge will grip on to the fabric. Following the directions in the kit, press the backing section into the button, making sure all the raw edges are hidden inside the button form.

To cover an existing button, you can use a similar technique, although this works only with shank buttons. Cut out a circle or fabric about 5mm (¼in) wider all round than the button. Run stitches round the edge of the circle as described above, but when you get to the end, keep the needle on the thread. Place the button, shank side up on the fabric and gather up the edges of the circle as described above. Then use the thread to make some secure stitches in the fabric to hold it tightly round the button shank.

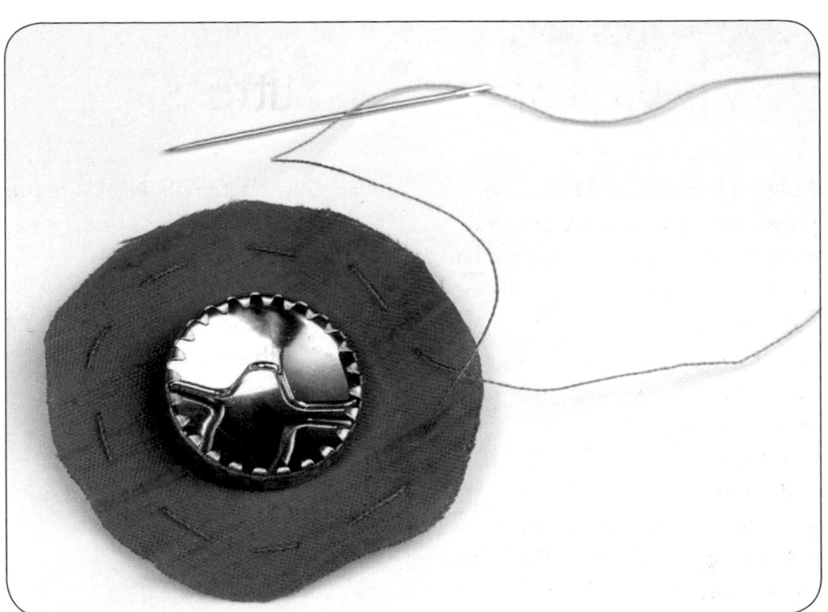

ABOVE After running gathering stitches around the fabric circle, place the button form, face side down, on the fabric.

ABOVE Gather up the stitches to draw the fabric into the middle of the form. Tuck the raw edges in before pushing the button-back in place.

Question 163:
I don't like the curved hemlines on shirts that are worn over trousers; can this be altered?

If you want to shorten the length of the shirt all round you can simply cut off the amount you want, straight across the bottom of the shirt and turn up a new hem all round; tailored shirts usually have 5mm (¼in) hems. But if you want to keep the length in the side seams,

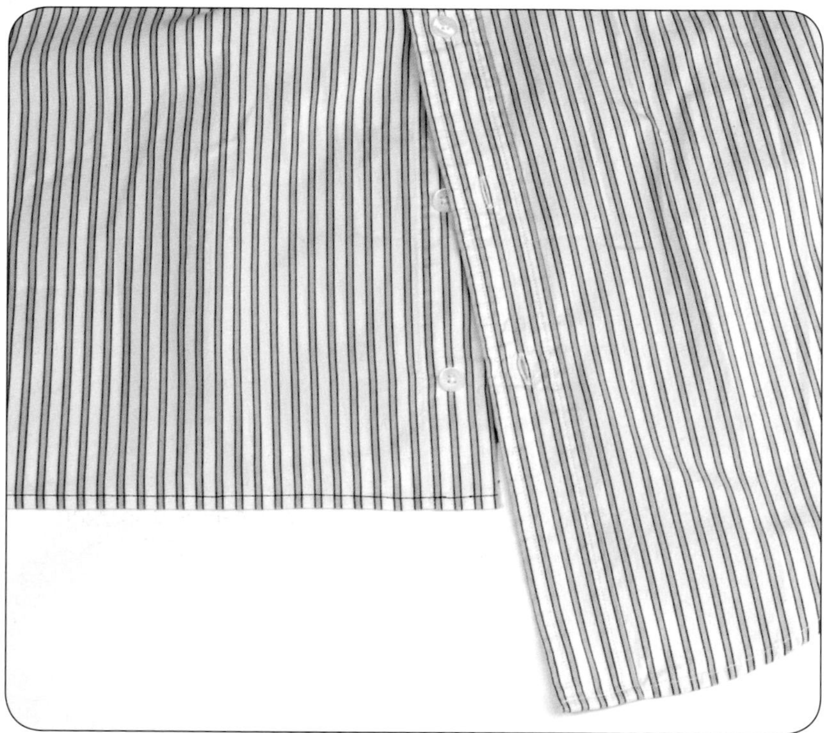

ABOVE If you don't want to keep the rather masculine look of a curved tail on a shirt, it is possible to cut this off and re-hem while still keeping the length in the sides.

you will have to remove just the curved section of the shirt.

Start by ripping out the original hem for about 10cm (4in) at each side seam. Fold the shirt in half lengthwise with the fold in the back centre. Pin the bottom edges together. Start cutting about 5cm (2in) from the side seam toward the fold in the back (be careful of the pins, they can put notches in your scissors), cutting off the shirt tail. Then, do the same about 5cm (2in) from the side seam towards the front of the shirt. Trim off any uneven edges. Try the shirt on again to make sure that it is even all around. The reason you should leave 5cm (2in) on both sides of the side seams is so that you will see the original hem in this area to begin your new hem.

Fold up the hem about 5mm (¼in) and then again about 1cm (½in) or narrower all round; pin. Sew the hem on the sewing machine and press well, using a pressing cloth.

Question 164:
T-shirts and knit tops are always too long for me; how can I shorten them?

Since t-shirt fabric will not fray, you can simply cut them to the length you like. If, however, you do not like the slightly unravelled edge this will create, you can simply turn under a new hem and stitch in place.

If you are machine stitching, use the correct sewing machine needle and a suitable thread, and do not stretch the fabric as you sew. Gently push the fabric along, not pulling it from the back of the sewing machine foot. If hand sewing, take wide spaced hemming stitches and do not pull the thread too tight.

Question 165:
How do I add a patch-style pocket to a garment?

This is another great way to add some creativity to garments, especially chrildren's clothes. Patch pockets can add a nice little touch to any sort of garment. They make a great practical addition to aprons, skirts and shirts.

To make patch pockets, you are simply sewing another piece of fabric on to something else very

ABOVE If you use a fabric for the patch pocket that's completely different to the rest of the garment, you'll create a decorative feature of this practical addition.

much as you would do a patch but with an opening at one side. Usually a patch pocket is lined or the edges are turned under so they will not fray. The patch pocket looks very much like a patch and, like patches, they can be any shape or size.

Decide on the size and shape of your pocket and add on 5mm (¼in) all round for allowances. Cut out one piece of your chosen fabric and one piece of lining to this size. (You could also use two pieces of the fabric instead of using lining.) The fabric should not be too heavy – about the same weight as the garment fabric. The lining will eliminate raw edges on the inside of the pocket. Pin the fabric and lining wrong sides together. Stitch all round, taking a 5mm (¼in) allowance and leaving a 5cm (2in) opening in the centre of one edge for turning. Clip off any corners and snip into any curves to eliminate bulk. Turn the patch pocket right sides out. Press well. Slip stitch the opening closed where you turned the pocket right side out. You can topstitch across the top edge of the pocket at this time, if you wish. Press again. Pin the side edges and the bottom edge of the patch pocket to your garment. Pin all the way around. Top stitch the pocket to the garment 3mm (⅛in) from the edge.

Question 166:
How do I keep my straight-leg trousers tucked into my boots?

Unless you have very slim or very tight trousers, your trousers are unlikely to stay tucked into your boots. The answer is to use temporary stirrups. You can buy clip-ons but I find the metal clasps uncomfortable. Another way is to make your own. You will need some elastic and two sets of larger size press studs for the first pair of trousers, and then one set of press studs the exact same size for any trousers you will be wearing with these same straps. Half of the press stud will go on to the elastic strap and the other half on to your trousers, which is why the press studs all need to be the same size.

Question 167:
How can I make these straps for all of my straight-leg trousers?

Try on your trousers. You'll need about 30cm (12in) of elastic for each foot. The elastic should be at least 1cm (½in) wide – no narrower or it will cut into the sole of your foot when you move.

Stepping on a measuring tape, measure the distance from your ankle bone on one side to the bone on the other side of the foot. Add another 5cm (2in) to this measurement. Usually there is no right or wrong side to elastic. Fold over the elastic about 2.5cm (1in) on each end. You will be sewing a press stud – half of the press stud – on to this folded area. Remember to fold down the elastic by the same amount at each end. The other half of the press stud will be sewn to the inside side seam allowance or hem at the side seams about 2.5cm (1in) from the bottom of the trousers.

It's not a problem if your trousers are not all the same length. Try on each pair of trousers and with the strap around the bottom of your foot, mark where the other half of the press stud should be sewn.

LEFT If you use press studs to make your elastic stirrups detachable, you will be able to wear your trousers without them whenever you wish.

Question 168: What are kimono and dolman sleeves?

In a garment with kimono sleeves, the sleeves and the body (or the yoke) of the garment are cut out as one piece. In other words, the sleeve is not a separate part, stitched into the armhole. A kimono sleeve is loose fitting and usually longer in the back.

A dolman sleeve is also cut as part of the bodice. It differs from a kimono sleeve in that it tapers, narrowing towards the wrist.

LEFT In this kimono-sleeved tunic top, the sleeves and the yoke are cut as one piece, with the ends of the sleeve turned up to form deep cuffs.

Question 169:
Is there any way to alter fuller-style sleeves?

The simplest way to alter fuller sleeves is to take in some of the fabric with darts. Turn the top inside out and take a tuck in the top of the sleeve near the shoulder until you have reduced the fullness as required; pin in place. If the garment has kimono or dolman sleeves, you should place your dart at the top of the shoulder, where the sleeve would join the bodice if it was a set-in type sleeve. Your dart will then look like the natural sleeve seam. This is also a great way to reduce the length of a sleeve without altering the wrist opening.

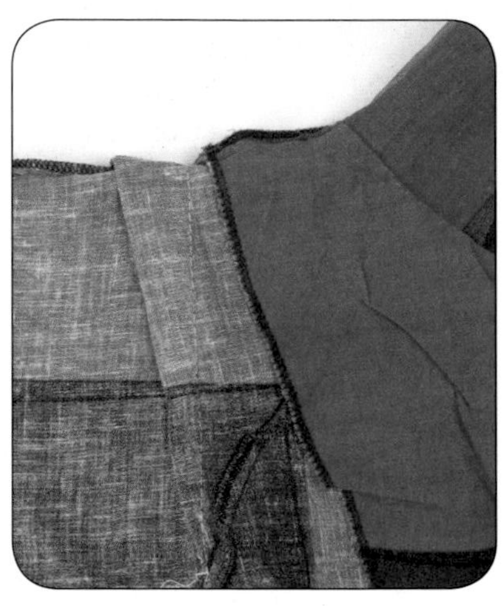

ABOVE Take a dart at the shoulder, tapering down towards the armhole.

Question 170:
How do I add a hood to a sweatshirt, jacket or coat?

A hood can be made of any fabric, but it's better if it is a similar fabric to the garment.

First you need to make a pattern. Measure round the neckline of what you want to add the hood to and halve this measurement. Using a photocopier or graph paper, enlarge the pattern shown here (right) until the bottom edge is the same as your measurement; since the edge is curved you will have to measure round with a tape measure and it may take a few tries at enlarging to get it right.

Then use your pattern to cut two pieces of fabric; cut them so the straight front edge of the hood pattern lines up with the fabric grain. Put the two pieces of fabric right sides together and stitch the centre back seam; finish the raw edges. Turn under the front edge of the hood to make a hem and stitch in place. If you want to add a drawstring, make sure the turning is deep enough to accommodate the width of your cord; leave the ends of the turning open but turn under and stitch the raw edges to ensure they don't fray. Cut a piece of cord long enough to go round the hood, plus at least 30cm (12in). Tie one end of the cord to a safety pin or bodkin and thread it through the turned edge of the hood. Knot each end of the cord to make sure it doesn't pull out.

Pin the remaining raw edge of the hood to the edge of your chosen garment. Tack in place and then try the garment on to make sure the hood is in the right place. When you are happy with the fit, stitch in place using zigzag stitch. For a neater finish, cover the new seam with binding.

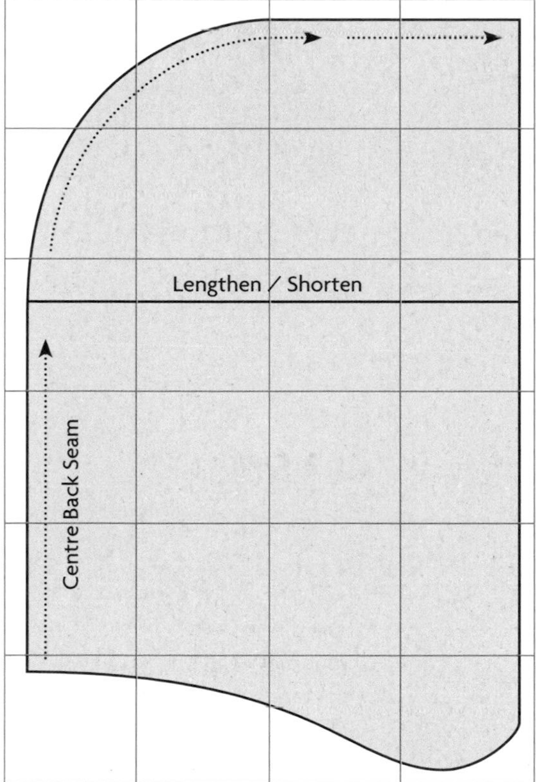

LEFT Scale this pattern up and use to cut two pieces of fabric. Lengthen or shorten your hood at the line indicated.

Question 171:
Can I make the hood detachable?

It's quite straightforward to make a detachable hood. Follow the instructions in Question 170 to make your hood and then, instead of stitching the hood to the garment, finish the raw edge of the hood – either with zigzag stitching or by hemming. Then pin the hood to the garment to see where you want it to be placed. When you are happy with the fit and position, take the garment off. Sew press studs around the collar and the edge of the hood. If the garment has a collar, sew the press studs underneath so they will not show.

Question 172:
Can I transform a long-sleeve T-shirt or sweatshirt into a cardigan?

It's easy to change a top into a casual cardigan; all you need to do is cut up the front and finish the edges. Before you begin, make sure that there is no pattern, design or pocket that goes across the garment front that you would be cutting in half. Also, you should not do this with a sweater that is tight fitting, unless you want it to permanently hang open.

Fold the top you want to alter in half at the centre front, matching side seams. Place a mark or pins every few inches along the fold. Unfold the garment and use a ruler to make sure you have marked a straight line; you do not want the opening to be crooked. Using the marks or pins as a guide, cut from top to bottom.

If you are cutting up a sweatshirt, you can fold under the front centre back and topstitch down – sweatshirts are knit and should not unravel. If you are cutting a knitted sweater, you need to finish off the raw edges. The best way to do this is to use some bias binding, which has some stretch. Stitch the binding to one of the cut edges, wrong sides together, then turn the binding to the right side and slip stitch in place. Repeat along the other cut edge. Turn the binding under at the top and bottom of the opening. A contrasting or a matching seam binding with a little shine can look very effective. You could also use the same binding to make ribbon ties. Cut two pieces of binding about 25cm (10in) long. Turn under one short edge on each piece and then fold each piece in half lengthways, wrong sides together. Topstitch around the edges of each piece. Stitch the raw end of one piece to the left-hand neck edge of the cardigan's opening; stitch the other piece to the right hand side.

ABOVE Once you've cut down the centre front of your garment you can finish the raw edges with bias binding.

173 What should I look for in charity shops and dress exchanges?

174 I have only basic mending skills; will I be able to fix or alter these clothes?

175 I love the fabric from a shirred-top summer dress, but I don't wear anything with straps; what can I do?

176 I found a fantastic jacket in a designer outlet, but it's the wrong size; is it possible to alter the fit?

177 I found a vintage blouse in a charity shop, but the seams are ripped under the arms; is there anything I can do?

178 I love the dress, but it's way too wide for my body; what are my options to alter it?

179 This dress needs a belt; can I do anything?

180 How can I add elastic in the back of a dress?

181 I've inherited a great vintage jacket but the fit is a bit tight; is there anything I can do?

182 How can I extend the life of my children's clothes?

183 How do I hem a girl's dress so she can wear it as she grows taller?

184 How do I make kids' trousers have cuffs that I can lengthen?

185 How do I eliminate an old hem line on the right side of a garment?

10

ADAPTING BARGAINS AND OTHER MONEY-SAVING IDEAS

Question 173:
What should I look for in charity shops and dress exchanges?

Charity shops are usually sponsored by a charity or other non-profit agency – such as Scope or Oxfam – and can sell clothes and other items very inexpensively. The clothes are usually well worn and much cheaper. However, I have purchased many bargains at these types of shop because many people are not familiar with or don't have the time to deal with a dress exchange, and so donate name-brand or designer clothes to these charity shops. On my last visit to a charity shop, I purchased an unworn pair of trousers, with the original price tag still on, for under £2. They may have been last season's or last year's style

ABOVE Charity shops sell a huge range of different garments. Search through their rails carefully and you may find a great bargain or an exciting vintage piece.

but with a small adjustment to the hem, they fit perfectly. I have found many other new or partly used clothes in thrift stores, but you do need to look carefully.

Dress exchanges are different. These outlets take your clothes for a specific period of time – maybe a month or two – and try to sell them. The amount achieved is then divided between you and the shop. If the garments remain unsold, you can pick them up again or the dress exchange may donate them to a charity.

There are some dress exchanges that sell only top quality, designer clothes and items. But there are many others with all types of clothing. I have purchased many wonderful bargains at these shops. Sometimes, if I want to try out a new fashion, I buy something very inexpensive and wear it to see how I feel. If I don't like it, I donate it or try to sell it to another dress exchange. These shops are the ideal places to look for quality bargains. And remember, you can use your new sewing skills to alter and adapt these garments to suit.

Question 174:
I have only basic mending skills; will I be able to fix or alter these clothes?

All you really need for most mending and simple alterations is very basic sewing skills. If it's a question of letting things down or taking them in, then you will find this easy to do with a good knowledge of basic stitches. And you don't need to be an expert to add creative touches and embellishments to your bargains. No complex techniques are required to add a trim or decorative detail. And if you want to attempt more advanced alterations to your clothes, then it's a great opportunity to take your basic skills a bit further. You might even find yourself enrolling in a sewing class!

Question 175: I love the fabric from a shirred-top summer dress, but I don't wear anything with straps; what can I do?

Recently, I was browsing in a dress exchange and I found a cotton skirt with an elastic waist that was about 30cm (12in) in width. I bought it and it was only when I got home, that I realised the skirt wasn't a skirt at all but had originally been a dress – the previous owner had cut off the straps.

You can do the same yourself and cut away the straps on a shirred-top dress. Just make sure you don't cut into the top of the dress – especially the elastic – and that you trim off any loose threads that might show. If the dress is too long to make a skirt, then you can easily hem it to the length you want.

ABOVE You can remove the straps on a shirred-top dress and turn it into a skirt. Sew press studs to the straps and dress and you can re-attach them when you want.

This is also a great way to extend the life of a child's summer dress if it has a similar elasticated top. The elastic will stretch to fit around the child's waist once the straps are cut away, and if the dress was long enough to start with, it may last a couple more years.

EXPERT TIP

"You could create a dual purpose outfit. If you cut the straps away carefully so they aren't shortened dramatically, you could stitch pres studs on to the dress and the end of the straps to re-attach when you want the skirt to become a dress again."

Question 176:
I found a fantastic jacket in a designer outlet, but it's the wrong size; is it possible to alter the fit?

To start with, if the jacket is too small then there is very little you can do to change this. You might be able to let down the hem if it's too short, but this is hard to do on a tailored garment. If it's too tight round the middle, then moving the buttons is a possibility.

If it's too big, then there are a variety of different alterations that you might be able to do. If it's too wide around the middle, then consider taking in the seams or adding appropriate darts. If it's too long, you can take up the hem at front and back. And if the sleeves are too wide or too long, you can take in the seams or take up the hems. You could also belt the jacket to take it in. Try making your own coordinating belt (see Question 160) and add chain loops to the jacket waist (see Question 161) to hold it in place.

Question 177:
I found a vintage blouse in a charity shop, but the seams are ripped under the arms; is there anything I can do?

Of course you can fix it, but before buying second-hand clothing, do check it very carefully. You may want that older vintage look but you wouldn't want an old yellowed top. Look under the arms; is the fabric stained here? If so, it's not really worth buying the top as such stains cannot be removed. But if the top is clean and only has some ripped seams, then buy it! However, do remember to wash it first before working on it.

Sewing underarm seams is just a matter or sewing several adjacent seams separately; the underarm is the point where three seams meet – the side seam of the bodice, the seam of the sleeve, and the seam between the top of the sleeve and the bodice.

Turn the blouse inside out and remove any loose threads from the old stitching. Trim off any ends and frayed edges of the fabric. Pin the bodice and sleeve seams together. Start with the sleeve seam and either machine stitch or backstitch along the seam, starting about 2.5cm (1in) before the rip begins and ending about 1.5cm (5⁄8in) from the end of the seam (or whatever the original seam allowance was). Turn the garment around and stitch along the bodice seam in the same way. Knot and cut the threads.

Then stitch the underarm seam, starting about 2.5cm (1in) before the rip begins. Stop when you get to the point where the bodice seam meets the sleeve seam. Turn the garment around and stitch the other side of the underarm seam in the same way, finishing at the same point. Knot and cut the thread at both lines of stitching. Make sure the intersection between all the seams is secure; you could make a few hand stitches here to be sure.

The assumption here is that all the seams at the underarm have ripped. If this is not the case, you can still use the same technique to fix those seams that have.

Question 178: I love the dress, but it's way too wide for my body; what are my options to alter it?

The easiest way to make a dress narrower is to take it in at the side seams. Turn it inside out and pin down the seams; start at the underarm and pin a seam that gradually widens until you get to the waistline, which then tapers to nothing at the hem. Try the dress on to make sure the fit is right before stitching the new seams in place.

You can also take in the back seam; simply follow the instructions for taking in the back seam of a blouse – see Question 143.

You can also adjust the size by using darts – either adding new darts or by increasing existing ones. A princess seam is an ideal way to take in the dress along its full length as this dart runs from shoulder to hem – see Question 141. If you want to take the dress in at the waist only, then make a dart that starts at the bust and goes down to the waist before ending at the hip. Make the dart start from nothing at the bust point and then widen out at the waist before narrowing to nothing again at the hip.

ABOVE One of the quickest and easiest ways to reduce a dress that is too wide is to take it in at the sides.

Question 179: This dress needs a belt; can I do anything?

The simplest option to this is, of course, to buy a suitable belt to go with the dress, and then make chain belt loops (see Question 161) to hold the belt in place. However, you could make a matching belt if there is enough fabric in the hem of your dress. Look at the hem on the inside of the garment, if there is at least 5cm (2in) of fabric turned under you could make a belt about 2.5cm (1in) wide. You will also need some interfacing and a fabric to back the belt; use a plain material that's the same weight as the dress fabric.

To do this, unpick the hem and turn it down. Press lightly so that the folded edge is still visible. Cut off the hem about 5mm (¼in) in from the fold. You need to rehem the dress so it's a good idea to do this straight away. Cut a piece of matching bias binding long enough to go round the hem. Pin the binding around the hem, right sides together, and machine stitch in place, following the fold in the binding. Fold the binding over to the wrong side and press. Pin in place all round and then hem the binding to the dress to create a false hem. You can now use the fabric that you cut off to make a belt.

If you've cut off the fabric in a continuous loop, cut along one of the original side seams to turn it into a strip. Press the strip. Cut out an identical sized strip in your backing fabric. Then cut a strip of fusible interfacing that is 5mm (¼in) less all round than both strips. Fuse the interfacing to the backing strip. Then follow the instructions for making a belt as described in Question 160.

If you don't have enough extra material in the dress to make a matching belt, you could consider using a contrasting fabric and make it up in the same way.

Question 180:
How can I add elastic in the back of a dress?

If you have a sway back, then adding some elastic to the back of a garment is a great way to get a good fit. First, try on your top or dress and pin exactly where you want the elastic. When the garment is gathered by the elastic, it will cause the garment to become shorter. So, if you are going to have to hem the garment, do so after the elastic has been added. If you are adding elastic around the whole garment, then the hem should be fine.

If you are only adding elastic to the very back of your garment, then you can simply sew it in place. Use a zigzag stitch and stretch the elastic as you stitch.

Alternatively, create a 'channel' known as a casing for the elastic to be pulled through. Choose some bias tape about 5mm (¼in) or 1cm (½in) wider than the elastic you wish to add to your dress. Measure across the back of your dress; cut a piece of bias tape about a third of this length. Turn under the short ends of the tape and stitch. Pin the bias tape to the inside of your dress, where you want the elastic to go, wrong side to wrong side and leaving each short end of the tape open. Machine stitch along the long edges of the tape. Attach one end of the elastic to a safety pin and thread it through the casing. Tack the other end of the elastic to the end of the bias tape and then pull on the safety-pin end to tighten the elastic and gather up the dress. Tack this end of the elastic into place. Make sure the fit is right and then stitch each end of the elastic in place securely.

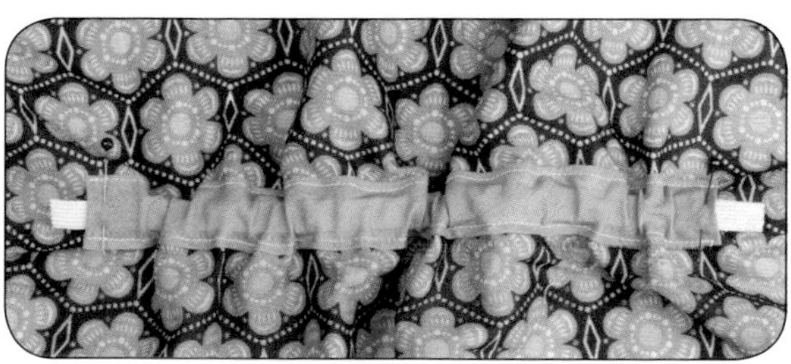

LEFT Thread the elastic through the casing and try on the dress. When you are happy with the fit, tuck the elastic inside the casing and stitch in place.

Question 181:
I've inherited a great vintage jacket, but the fit is a bit tight; is there anything I can do?

If the fit is tight round the arms, you could turn a jacket into a waistcoat. You will need to take the sleeves off and, possibly, make the armholes a little wider. Don't throw the sleeves away – you may be able to use the fabric to make covered buttons or re-use in another project.

First, carefully separate the sleeves from the jacket. If the jacket and sleeves are lined, also separate the lining. If the armholes are too small, you can cut them wider; start by taking off about 5mm (¼in) all around the armhole. Try on the garment, if you need the armholes bigger, try another 5mm (¼in). Remember to do the same alterations on both armholes.

If the jacket was lined, turn in the edges of the armholes in the lining all the way around. Sew by hand or topstitch by machine. If it wasn't lined, you can simply turn under the armhole edges and machine sew them down. If you are worried that the fabric will fray, before turning under and sewing the edges, zigzag the raw edges. You do not need a tight zigzag to do this.

Question 182:
How can I extend the life of my children's clothes?

As we all know, children can grow taller in a matter of weeks so buying new clothes this frequently is not really practical. And as they shoot up, they often just get taller, rather than wider. It's possible, therefore, to lengthen their clothes and extend the amount of time they can be worn. The simplest way is to let down the existing hem. Better quality children's clothing often has deeper hems, so this can be a practical option.

First unpick the hem using a seam ripper. Then unfold the old hem and remove any loose stitches and threads that remain. Press well. If the old hem still has a 5mm (¼in) turning, you can retain this. If not, either turn up the raw edge of the fabric or finish with zigzag stitch if necessary. Turn under the shortest hem possible and pin. Press and then hem stitch in place.

Question 183: How do I hem a girl's dress so she can wear it as she grows taller?

First of all, start by buying your child a dress that is longer than needed. You will then take tucks at the bottom of the dress, much in the way that you do when making French hems for jeans (see Question 129). The difference here is that you will not cut away the excess fabric in the tucks; as the girl grows, you simply let down one tuck after another. If the tucks leave a mark, simply cover with a length of ribbon or decorative binding.

You could make a feature of the tucks themselves. Instead of concealing the tucks on the inside of the garment (as you would for the French hem), make them on the right side. Make them evenly spaced and make each one the same size. Press them down towards the hem to create a ridged effect.

ABOVE If you put your tucks in on the right side of the dress, the effect of the overlapping folds can be pretty in itself.

Question 184:
How do I make kids' trousers have cuffs that I can lengthen?

When you buy trousers for children, buy them longer than needed. Fold up the hem a few times, press well and hem. As your child grows taller you can take down each fold. If the folded layers are too thick to hem, stitch-in-the-ditch on the side seams. Stitch the rolled up hem down the side seams. When your child needs the trousers to be let down, you can take out these stitches, unfold the hem the extra amount you need, then either hem stitch or stitch-in-the-ditch again at the new length.

An alternative is to give the trousers adjustable cuffs. You fold the ends up and hold them in place with lengths of seam binding or ribbon, attached with press studs.

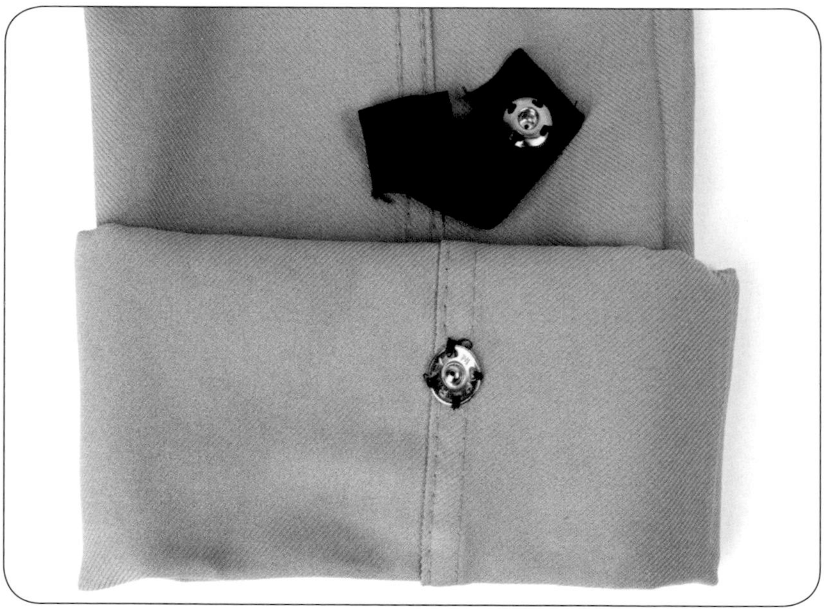

ABOVE You can turn up a cuff on kids' trousers and use a length of tape and a press stud to hold it in place; turn it down (repositioning the press stud) as required.

Fold up the trousers to the desired length, either toward the inside or outside. Measure the depth of the fold and double it. Cut two lengths of seam binding or ribbon to this measurement plus about 1cm (½in) to turn under the ends. Mark where the edge of the folded cuff comes on the seam and stitch one half of a press stud in this position; stitch the other half to one end of a piece of binding. Turn the trouser leg to the inside and sew another press stud to the inside of the seam, in the same position as the outside press stud. Stitch the other half of this press stud to the other end of the binding. Repeat for the other leg. Fold up the trousers to make the cuff and then hold this in place with the seam binding. As the child grows and the cuff needs to be shorter, simply move the press studs down the leg.

Question 185:
How do I eliminate an old hem line on the right side of a garment?

Sometimes when a garment has been washed frequently and placed in the dryer many times, the original hem line is set in and still shows when the hem is let down, however much you iron or steam a garment.

You could try this fix: make up a mixture of one part vinegar to three parts water and put this in a spray bottle; shake well to mix. Spray the mixture on the hem line and place a pressing cloth on top. Press, using a hot steam setting if the fabric of your garment allows.

If all else fails, you could simply add some decoration to cover the old hem line. Choose some suitable ribbon or a length of ric-rac.

186 Can I use my new-found skills to mend things other than clothes?

187 What can I do with those itchy labels in my shop-bought clothes?

188 I just got a new job but all I have in my wardrobe are t-shirts; how can I make them look nicer for the office?

189 How can I make easy decorative flowers to trim clothes?

190 How can I make a plain sweater look dressier?

191 How can I decorate with buttons?

192 How do I add a fringe to the edge of a dress or skirt?

193 How can I add a trim to cuffs?

194 My pillowcases are beginning to rip at the seams; how can I fix these?

195 I would love to hand down a cherished crocheted blanket, but the edges are frayed; what can I do?

196 My windows are shorter than the standard length; how can I shorten curtains to fit?

197 How do I lengthen ready-made curtains?

198 My tablecloth has several noticeable stains; can I transform it into something else?

199 My favourite tablecloth is fraying round the hem; how can I fix this?

200 How can I make placemats look more coordinated with my tablecloth?

11

TAKING YOUR SEWING SKILLS FURTHER

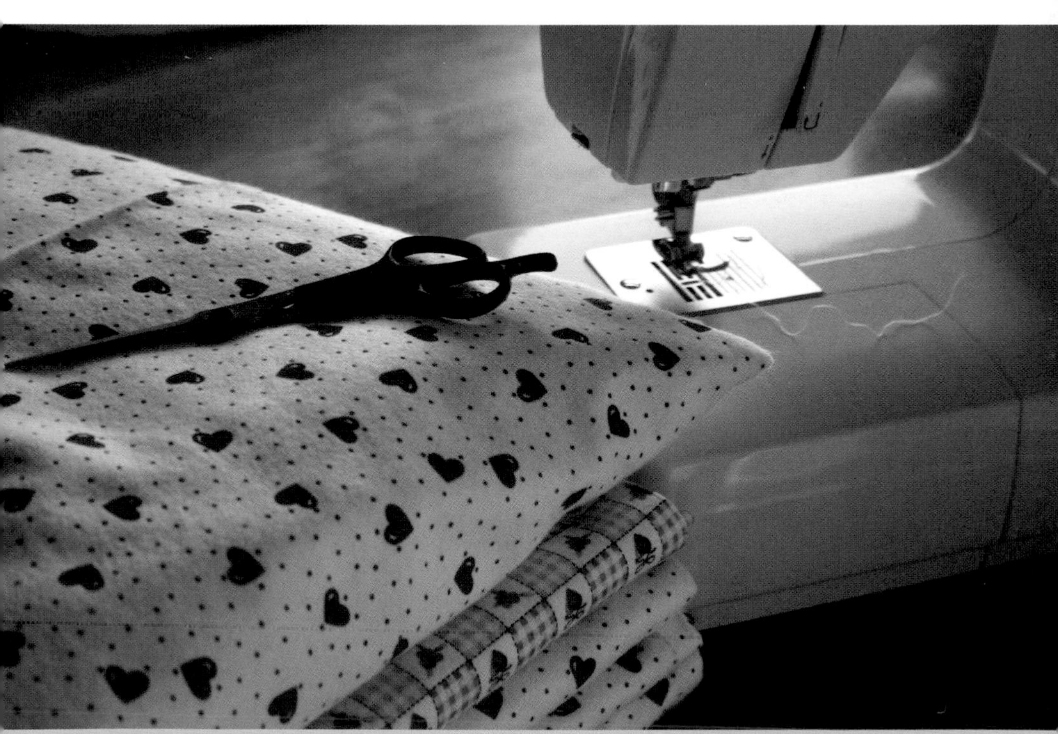

Question 186:
Can I use my new-found skills to mend things other than clothes?

In this book, you have already learned the basics of mending and altering clothes and there is no reason why you can't apply these skills to do almost any other kind of household sewing. You can repair tears and holes in bed and table linens, fix pillows that have burst open, mend curtain hems that have come down, sew handles back on to bags – the list is endless.

You will also be able to adapt and embellish your home furnishings to give them a new lease of life. Trims and other decoration can just as easily be added to linens, throws, pillows and other household items as they can to clothing.

Question 187:
What can I do with those itchy labels in my shop-bought clothes?

First, read what is on the labels. Some years ago, manufacturers began to change the location of the cleaning and fabric content labels to low down in the side seams where they are less irritating to your skin. However, not all manufacturers stick to this and you may find the care labels still sewn into the neckline. And to be honest, the retailer's own label can still be an irritant.

Some labels are stitched in using a plastic thread. This can melt slightly in the dryer or during ironing and can cause a sharp end on the thread that might be what is irritating you. If a label is sewn in this way, you can, carefully, with very sharp scissors or a seam ripper, take the plastic stitching out. If you want, sew the label back on with ordinary thread. However, do you really need the label? If it features care instructions, then keep the label somewhere safe and refer to it whenever you wash the garment.

ABOVE When unpicking the label from a garment, take care to cut only through the stitches holding the label in place, and not through the garment stitching.

Alternatively, sew the care label back into the side seam.

When taking out a label sewn on with ordinary thread, take care when unpicking the stitches to make sure you don't cut any important stitching or any of the fabric – particularly if removing a label from a knitted garment. Sometimes the label is inserted in a seam or under a turned edge and then incorporated into the garment stitching. If you remove labels like these, the edge or seam will unravel.

Question 188:
I just got a new job but all I have in my wardrobe are T-shirts; how can I make them look nicer for the office?

Simple T-shirts of all types are the staple of any wardrobe. I don't mean large T-shirts bearing advertising slogans and bold motifs, I'm talking about solid-colour, fitted T-shirts that can be worn tucked into trousers, skirts and under jackets for the office.

Most of these type of T-shirts are just plain, but these ordinary garments can be easily adapted to make them look so much nicer. All you need to do is add some subtle embellishment. Try stitching on some decorative buttons, ribbons, or little flowers.

Question 189:
How can I make easy decorative flowers to trim clothes?

Making little flowers out of fabric to decorate clothing is incredibly easy. A lightweight fabric will work best and you don't have to worry about finishing off the raw edges as a frayed edge will add to the look of the finished flower. You can match the fabric to the clothing you want to decorate, or you can pick a contrasting material.

Find something circular – a jar lid, for example – that is about 5cm (2in) in diameter and use it to draw two circles on your chosen fabric. Cut the circles out. With a needle and single thread in a matching colour make small stitches all the way around each circle, about half way between the centre point and the edge of the fabric. Pull on the thread to gather up the stitches, but not so much that the flower will not lie flat. A little 'bubble' will form in the centre of the flower. Knot and tie the thread and

ABOVE It's easy to make decorative flowers out of scraps of fabric. Stitch them to the neckline of a plain t-shirt to give it a new lease of life.

cut. Do the same with the second circle. Place one circle on top of the other, bubble down. If one is bigger, place the smaller one on top. Sew the two together, stitching a small bead or button at the centre.

You can make larger or small flowers, make flowers out of three or four circles of fabric or make flowers out of circles that get progressively wider. You could even use more than one fabric.

Question 190:
How can I make a plain sweater look dressier?

A single-coloured, plain sweater can look dull but there are plenty of ways to add a bit of excitement. You can, of course, consider any of the options discussed elsewhere in this chapter; adding fringes, stitching on buttons or creating fabric flowers. One decoration that looks effective on knitwear is to add a flat type of trim that adds a contrast to the fluffiness of the knit.

Choose something that stands out against the colour of your sweater; if the trim is dull or matches the garment, it won't have the desired effect. Decide where you want to add the trim; the neckline and wrists are probably perfect places to add embellishment. Measure your garment to find out how much trim you need and then cut to length, adding extra if you need to turn the edges under. Pin to the garment and then stitch in place using a thread that matches the trim, not the sweater. Make your stitches small and unobtrusive.

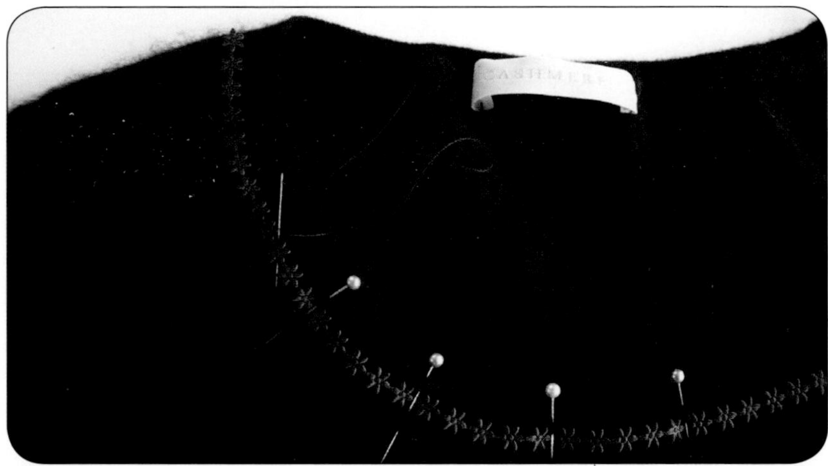

ABOVE Pin your chosen trim round the neckline of a sweater and then make small stitches, using a thread that matches the trim, to secure in place.

Question 191:
How can I decorate with buttons?

Buttons don't have to be boring! They can be used to add a decorative touch as well as to fasten your clothing. A lot of buttons are pretty in their own right but you can still use a plain button to add decoration; simple pearl buttons can look just as good if combined with other shaped buttons or if grouped together to make a shape, such as a flower or a heart.

Why not use several small round buttons to make a heart shape on the front of a t-shirt? Or mix together several different types of buttons and stitch around a neckline. You could also add purely decorative buttons to a cuff or around the wrist.

Since you'll need fewer buttons for decoration than you would to fasten a garment, you may find just what you're looking for in your button stash. Or you may find a store that sells buttons singly, rather than in multiples. Don't forget to look for interesting buttons on old garments in charity shops and second-hand stores; it may be worth paying a bit extra for the clothing if the buttons are special enough!

ABOVE A selection of small but pretty buttons can add a decorative touch to any plain garment. You can use either matching or contrasting thread to stitch in place.

Question 192:
How do I add a fringe to the edge of a dress or skirt?

Adding a fringe to the bottom edge of a dress or skirt is really very simple, and there are many different decorative trims available in the stores. Measure all round the hem and cut your fringe to this length plus a bit extra to overlap.

Turn the dress or skirt to the wrong side and pin the fringe in place. Turn back to the right side and make sure the fringe protrudes as much as you want. Then tack the fringe in place.

Thread a needle with a single thread that matches the garment. Knot the thread and secure at the wrong side of the garment; it's a good idea to start off at one of the side seams. Then bring the needle through to the right side. Stitch the trim in place all round the hem, working on the right side. Make your stitches small on the right side so they don't show; they can be longer on the wrong side.

ABOVE A multi-coloured fringe can completely transform a plain skirt.

Question 193:
How can I add a trim to cuffs?

You can trim cuffs in the same way as adding a fringe to a skirt or dress hem (see Question 192). You can choose to add a fringe, but you can also add a length of gathered lace trim using the same method.

Another way to decorate cuffs is to sew the trim directly on the cuff. If you buy ready-made trims or ribbons, you do not need to do any type of edge finishing, they are ready to sew on as they are. On narrow trims, you can simply stitch down the centre of the trim to secure. On wider trims, stitch close to both edges.

By using trims on cuffs you can help coordinate different garments. For example, if your child has a plain jacket and several different coloured pairs of trousers, add a few rows of trim to the jacket cuffs that are the same colour as the trousers. Each time he or she wears the jacket and any of the trousers, they will look like a matching set.

You can also use trims on cuffs to cover up any stains, holes or worn areas, as well as to cover up any old hem lines that are visible after lengthening sleeves.

Question 194:
My pillowcases are beginning to rip at the seams; how can I fix these?

Pillowcases have straight seams and so are easy to mend. Turn the pillowcase inside out and trim off any loose threads. Pin the ripped seam. Stitch along the seam, beginning about 2.5cm (1in) from where it is ripped, and finishing about 2.5cm (1in) after the rip.

Pillowcases have an overlapped section at one end; this is where the pillow is tucked to hold it in place. If the seam is ripped beyond the point where the overlap ends, you will have to incorporate this into the mended seam too.

Question 195:
I would love to hand down a cherished crocheted blanket, but the edges are all frayed; what can I do?

The best way to fix this is to bind the edges with a fabric. You can use a strip of fabric, or use blanket seam binding or ribbon. The advantage of the latter two is that you will not have to turn under the edges.

Measure all round the edges of the blanket and then add on at least 20cm (8in) for mitring the corners and overlapping the ends to get the length of your binding. If you are cutting a binding out of fabric, decide on how deep you want the trim and double this. Add on 2.5cm (1in) for turned edges. Cut your fabric to this width by the length you have already calculated.

ABOVE Use a good quality, long-lasting fabric to bind the edges of your blanket.

If you are binding the blanket with fabric, turn under the long edges on the fabric strip by 1cm (½in); press. Whatever your choice of binding, fold it in half lengthways and press. Fold the binding over the edge of the blanket and pin in place. At the corners you can fold the binding into neat mitred points – fold the excess fabric into a diagonal line and tuck in with the binding. If the corners of the blanket are rounded, you can gather the binding into small tucks as you bend it round the corners. Tack in place to secure.

When you get to the end of pinning the binding round the blanket, turn under the narrow edge of the binding and overlap the starting point; pin. If you are using a fabric binding, stitch it in place on both sides of the blanket using slip stitch; join the overlapping ends with slip stitch. For blanket binding or ribbon, use small running stitches or an embroidery stitch like herringbone. Alternatively, use a zigzag machine stitch.

Question 196:
My windows are shorter than the standard length; how can I shorten curtains to fit?

To hem curtains, you will be making a simple hem by folding up, turning under the raw edges and topstitching the hem down. If the curtains are long enough, you can leave a hem that is 10–12.5cm (4–5in) deep.

The hem of a curtain plays a vital part in how a curtain hangs. Most curtains rely on the weight of the hem to hang properly. A deeper (wider) hem weighs down the curtains and lets them hang better. The lighter the weight of the curtain fabric, the wider the hem you will need. A sheer fabric may need a 12.5cm (5in) hem.

Hang your curtains in the window for which they are intended. Decide where you want the curtains to end and place a horizontal line of pins across each curtain to mark this point; the curtains need to hang down below the window sill. Do this with both curtains at the same time: don't hang up one curtain and presume you will be doing the same alteration on the other one – your curtain rail may not be straight and the curtains may not hang evenly, so it's best to get the new hem marked on each one.

Take the curtains down and measure down from the line of pins to the depth you need the new hem. Mark this point. If you are making short curtains from very long ones, then you will need to cut the excess fabric off. However, if you are shortening by just a small amount, then just make a wider hem. If you've trimmed off any fabric, turn under the raw edge and machine stitch. Then turn up the new hem so that marker pins are along the folded edge. Using a hemming stitch, hem the curtains.

If the curtains are lined, you will have to unpick the lining at the sides slightly and then turn under the same amount as the hem. Remember, the lining is shorter than the curtain so it does not protrude under the curtain edge. Since the lining does not show on the right side of the curtain, you can machine stitch this hem in place. Using slip stitch, re-sew the lining in place.

Question 197:
How do I lengthen ready-made curtains?

To lengthen curtains, you'll need to be a little bit more creative. Before doing any sewing alterations, first do a few easy checks. Measure the length of the curtains, and compare with the length of the windows. Is the difference only a small amount? Is it possible to move the curtain rod or rail down the wall this amount? Lowering the curtain fixtures and fittings will make curtains appear longer.

If this is not possible, check out the hem of the curtains; can it be let down and then taken up again as a narrower hem?

If none of these options is possible, you can also lengthen the curtains by adding in a horizontal band of additional fabric. You can sew the fabric to the bottom of the curtains or cut the curtain in two and insert the fabric band before sewing the bottom of the curtain back on (in this way, you do not need to rehem the curtains).

Choose a colour or print that goes well with the curtain fabric or that coordinates with something else in the room. You should also choose a fabric that is the same weight as the curtains. A lightweight fabric will be dragged out of shape by the weight of the existing curtain fabric, and too heavy a weight of fabric and the lengthened curtain won't hang well.

Measure the width of the curtain, including the turned edges at the side. This will be the width of your band. Work out how much you need to add to the length and add on 3cm (1¼in) for the seams. This will be the depth of the band. Cut the fabric band to these dimensions.

Cut across the curtain at the point where you want to insert the band. Unpick the side hems a little way. Pin the fabric band to one of the cut edges of the curtain, right sides together, and stitch, making a 1.5cm (⅝in) seam allowance. Pin the other edge of the fabric band to the remaining cut edge of the curtain and stitch this seam in the same way. Finish the raw edges and press the seam allowances downwards. Turn under the side hems of the curtains and restitch in place.

Question 198:
My tablecloth has several very noticeable stains; can I transform it into something else?

If you are absolutely sure that the stain cannot be removed, you can cut the tablecloth – cutting around the stains – into smaller items, such as a smaller tablecloth, placemats or even cloth napkins.

To make placemats, cut round a piece of card cut to the shape you want or use an old placemat as a template. Placemats need to be thick so cut out a backing fabric from a coordinating material. Place the two layers wrong sides together and tack together. Then sew seam binding or bias binding around around the raw edges of the placemats to finish.

To make napkins is even simpler. Cut squares or rectangles to the size you want and then simply hem all round the edges, folding the fabric neatly at the corners. Alternatively, trim the raw edges with binding and then use the same binding to create coordinating cloth napkin rings.

ABOVE You can cut your tablecloth into napkins; trim the edges with bias binding and use a matching piece to make a napkin ring.

Question 199:
My favourite tablecloth is fraying round the hem; how can I fix this?

First cut off all the fraying threads. Then turn up a new hem all round, folding in all the frayed edges. Be aware, however, that this will make the tablecloth a bit smaller all the way around.

Alternatively, you can purchase or make some matching or coordinating binding. You can use seam binding to finish the edges of a square or rectangular tablecloth but bias binding will be better for a round cloth since the stretch in the binding will make it possible to ease the binding round the curved edge.

ABOVE Trim the frayed edges of your tablecloth with a plain or printed binding that coordinates with the colour of the tablecloth.

Question 200:
How can I make placemats look more coordinated with my tablecloth?

To make placemats coordinate with your tablecloth and maybe napkins you need to add some trimming that will help bring the different elements together. A good way to do this is to pick out a colour that either features in all three items of table linen, or that will match each item. You can then find a fabric or a binding of that colour and use it to decorate the placemats, tablecloth and napkins. If you are lucky, you might be able to find a patterned material that coordinates with

ABOVE If you can trim a bit off your tablecloth, you can use it to decorate your placemats and create a matching set.

each item. You can use the binding around the edges or you can stitch it across the ends of each item.

Alternatively, make the placemats double sided. Cut out a piece of your coordinating fabric a little bigger all round than the placemat. Turn under the raw edges and pin the fabric to the back of the placemat; secure with slip stitch. You can then choose which side to have on display. If you make napkin rings out of the same fabric, you will be able to link the napkins in to the same scheme.

If you've got a particularly large tablecloth and you don't mind losing some of the length, you can cut a bit off and use this to trim your placemats and napkins. They'll be a perfect match!

Index

A-line skirts 136-7
armhole openings 116

back darts 156
backstitch 47, 52, 97
beeswax 24
belts
  adding belt loops to a garment 179
  and hems 100
  making matching 178, 200
bias binding 119, 120, 191, 200
blanket stitch 47, 53, 63
blouses 146, 152
bodices 116
bodkins 24
buttonholes 63
buttons 56-64
  changing 176
  collections of 57, 176
  covering holes in knits with 86
  creativity with 56
  decorating with 213
  extra 25
  garment not hanging flat after sewing on 68
  making covered 180-1
  moving on jackets 160-1
  sewing on buttons 58-9
    with shanks 62
  sew-through 56, 61
  shank 56, 60-2

canvas needlework kits 18
cardigans
  transforming sweaters into 190-1
catch stitch 47, 50
charity shops 6-7, 194-5
children
  age to start teaching to sew 17
  cuffs for lengthening on trousers 204-5
  extending the life of children's clothes 202-3
  hemming a dress for a growing girl 203
  knotting thread 41
  sewing projects for 18-19
closed-ended zips 76
coats
  adding hoods to 188-90
  buttons 61, 64, 176
  changing collars or cuffs 176
coil zippers 76
collars 116
  changing 176
colours of thread 36, 37, 38, 46
cotton
  ironing 124, 129
  thread 34
cotton-wrapped polyester thread 34, 35
covered buttons 180-1
cuffs 116
  adding trim to 215
  changing 176
  shortening cuffed sleeves 166-7
curtains 217-18

darning 86-7
darning eggs 87
darts 146-7
  altering tops with 154-6
  at the waist 147
  shoulder seams 170
decorative trims 92, 210-14
detachable hoods 190
dolmen sleeves 187
double thread 40, 43
dress exchanges 6-7, 195
dresses
  adding elastic in the back of 201
  adding fringes to 213
  altering maternity dresses 173
  bodices of 116
  hemming 101
    for a growing girl 203
  making narrower 199
  shirred-top 196-7
  taking in at the sides 158
  transforming into tunic-like tops 177
dressmaking shears 27

elastic
  adding in the back of a dress 201
elasticated waistbands 147-9
  adding elastic to the back of 148
  putting darts in 147
  replacing the old elastic in 149
  taking out fullness in skirts 138
elastic thread
  sewing buttons with 64
embroidery scissors 27

fabric
  interfacings 117
  ironing different fabrics 124, 129-30
  linings 118
  right side of 22
  thread colour to match 38
  underlinings 118
facings 116
flowers, trimming clothes with fabric 210-11
four-holed buttons 59
frayed hems/edges 105, 216, 220
fraying buttonholes 63
French hemming 143-5
French seams 93
front darts 155
fusible webbing 90

garments
  parts and pieces of 116-17

half backstitch 52
hand mending 10, 13, 83-107
  basic skills 12, 195
  benefits from learning 15, 16
  hems 98-107
  knitted garments 84-7
  needles for 33
  patching 88-92
  pockets 97
  seams 93-7
  sewing terms 22
  supplies for 23-5
haute couture clothes 29
hemming stitch 47, 49, 103
hems 22, 98-107
  cuffs for lengthening on children's trousers 204-5
  eliminating old hem lines 205
  hemming
    curtains 217
    a dress for a growing girl 203
    leather 107
    linings 104
    shirts 182-3
  letting down 99
  longer at the back 106
  machine-sewn 98
  mending a frayed hem 105
  narrow circumference 104
  preparing for hemming 100
  stitching 47, 49, 102, 103
  turning up 101
  wide circumference 102-3
  width of 98
history of sewing 10
holes
  in knitted garments 86
  patching 88-92
Hong Kong seams 93, 118
hoods 188-90
hook-and-eye closures 69-74
  making a loop for a hook 73
  sewing on 70-2

interfacings 117
  replacing old 165
ironing 124-33
  different fabrics 129-4
  taking out scorch marks 130
irons
  cleaning 132-3
  spitting 131

jackets
  adding hoods to 188-90
  altering fit of 197, 202
  altering lined jackets 163
  buttons on
    changing 176
    moving 160-1
    shank buttons 61
  changing collars or cuffs 176
  taking in loose 162-3
jeans
  French hemming 143-5
  patching 88
  turning into shorts 143

kimono sleeves 187
knits 22, 84-7
  darning 86-7
  ironing wool 129
  making sleeves narrower 167
  mending holes in 86
  mending seams 97
  snags on 85
  supplies for mending 84
knotting thread 18

labels, taking out 208-9
leather, hemming 107
linen
  ironing 129
linings 118
  altering lined skirts 137
  hemming 104
  in jackets 163
  in sleeves 164-5

maternity dresses 173
money-saving ideas 13, 194-205

napkins and placemats 219, 220-1
necklines
  fixing stretched 172
  openings 116
  taking up 153
needles
  for children 17, 18
  eye of the needle 22
  holding while sewing 32
  sewing machine 112
  threading 18, 30
  type and size for hand mending 33
needle-threaders 24, 31
nylon thread 34

open seams 94, 96
overcast stitch 47, 53
overlocked seams 94, 96, 115
overlockers 45

patching 88-92
  adding decorative stitching to 92
  attaching a patch to a garment 91
  buying patches 89
  home-made patches 92
  making your own patches 90
patch pockets 184-5
pillowcases 215
pin cushions 26
pinking shears 27
pins 26
placemats 219, 220-1
pockets 97
  adding patch-style 184-5
polyester thread 34, 36
pressing 126
  hems 103
press studs 65-8
  ball and socket 65
  on infant and baby clothes 65
  sewing on 67
  when to use 66
pressing cloths 127, 130
pressing hams 128
princess seams 146, 157

ready-made clothes 16

scissors 27
seam allowances 22, 93, 97
  and zips 79
seam binding 118, 120-1
seams 93-7
  finishing off edges 45
  fixing ripped 95, 198
  fixing tears in seam closures 96-7
  ripping out machine-stitched 114
  ripping out overlocked 115
sergers 45
sewing
  age to start teaching 17
  by hand or machine 29
  history of 10
sewing kits 35
sewing machines 10, 28-9, 110-13
  accessories and needles for 112
  attachments 113
  choosing 110
  edging/piping foot 148
  thread for 37, 113
  using 110-11
sew-through buttons 56, 58-9, 61
shank buttons 56, 60-2
shirts
  hemming 182-3
shorts, turning jeans into 143
shoulder pads 171
shoulders, taking up 170
silk
  ironing 129
  pins for 26
skirts 136-8
  adding fringes to 213
  darts in 146
  hemming 100, 101, 102-3
  parts of 116
sleeves 164-70
  altering fuller-style 188
  dolmen/kimono 187
  making narrower around the wrist 167
  shortening 164-7
  taking up shoulders in 170
slip stitch 47, 51
Spandex 22
stitching
  basic sewing stitches 47-53
  ending 43
  hems 102, 103
  ripping out 44, 99
  securing thread 42
  topstitching 46, 93
  using an overlocker 45
  on zips 77
sweaters
  adding decorative trims 212
  transforming into cardigans 190-1
sweatshirts
  adding hoods to 188-90

tablecloths 219-21
tacking stitch 47, 48
tailors 13, 14
tailor's chalk 24
thread 34-43
  colours 36, 37, 38, 46
  different types of 34-6
  double 40, 43
  elastic 64
  ending the stitching 43
  for hand mending 34, 35, 39
  knotting 18, 41
  length of 39
  making a loop for a hook from 73

securing stitches 42
for sewing machines 37, 113
sizes 37
stitching hems 102
threading needles 18, 30
tops 152-60
adding a pleat to the centre back 160
custom-fitting 154
neckline alterations 116, 153, 172
princess seams 157
shortening knit tops 183
taking in at the sides 158
taking in the back seam 159
taking up the shoulders 170
transforming dresses into tunic-like tops 177
using darts to alter 154-6
topstitched seams 93, 94, 96
topstitching 46
trousers 139-42
adding elastic to the back of 148
adjusting the crotch depth 139, 140
darts in 146
hemming 100, 101, 102-3
longer at the back 106
hook and eye fastenings 70, 74
making elastic stirrups for 185-6
parts of 116
taking in legs of 141
turning long into cropped 142
T-shirts
adding decorative trims 210-11
necklines 172
shortening 183
two-holed buttons, sewing on 58

velvet 129

waistbands
darts at 147
elasticated 147-9
grown-on 116
hook and eye fastenings 70, 74
wovens 22
wrist openings 116

zips 75-81
parts and construction of 75
problems with 76, 77
pulls 81
stuck 77, 80-1
tearing away from fabric 79
teeth catching 78
types of 76

Acknowledgments

~~cover iStock~~; 2–14 Shutterstock; 15 iStock; 16–17 Shutterstock; 19 iStock; 21 Shutterstock; 22–26 Quantum Publishing (Marcos Bevilacqua); 27–28 iStock; 30–33 Quantum Publishing (Marcos Bevilacqua); 35–37 Shutterstock; 38–44 Quantum Publishing (Marcos Bevilacqua); 45 Getty Images/Peter Anderson; 46–53 Quantum Publishing (Marcos Bevilacqua); 55 Shutterstock; 57–60 Quantum Publishing (Marcos Bevilacqua); 61 Shutterstock; 62–65 Quantum Publishing (Marcos Bevilacqua); 66 Getty Images/Peter Anderson; 67–80 Quantum Publishing (Marcos Bevilacqua); 83 Shutterstock; 84–87 Quantum Publishing (Marcos Bevilacqua); 88 iStock; 89 Quantum Publishing (Marcos Bevilacqua); 91 Quantum Publishing (Caroline Dear); 92 Quantum Publishing (Marcos Bevilacqua); 93 Shutterstock; 94–97 Quantum Publishing (Marcos Bevilacqua); 98 iStock; 99–106 Quantum Publishing (Marcos Bevilacqua); 109 Shutterstock; 111 iStock; 112 Quantum Publishing (Marcos Bevilacqua); 114 Getty Images/Peter Anderson; 115–117 Quantum Publishing (Marcos Bevilacqua); 119 Getty Images/Peter Anderson; 120–121 Quantum Publishing (Marcos Bevilacqua); 123 Shutterstock; 125 iStock; 127–126 Quantum Publishing (Marcos Bevilacqua); 131 Shutterstock; 132 iStock; 135–137 Shutterstock; 138–140 Quantum Publishing (Caroline Dear); 141 Quantum Publishing (Marcos Bevilacqua); 142 Quantum Publishing (Caroline Dear); 145 (all) Quantum Publishing (Marcos Bevilacqua); 146 Shutterstock; 151 Shutterstock; 152–156 Quantum Publishing (Marcos Bevilacqua); 157 Shutterstock; 159–161 Quantum Publishing (Caroline Dear); 162–171 Quantum Publishing (Marcos Bevilacqua); 173 iStock; 175 Shutterstock; 176–186 Quantum Publishing (Marcos Bevilacqua); 187 Shutterstock; 188 Quantum Publishing (Marcos Bevilacqua); 191 Quantum Publishing (Caroline Dear); 192–194 Shutterstock; 196 Quantum Publishing (Marcos Bevilacqua); 199 Quantum Publishing (Caroline Dear); 201–204 Quantum Publishing (Marcos Bevilacqua); 207 Shutterstock; 209–213 Quantum Publishing (Caroline Dear); 214 Quantum Publishing (Marcos Bevilacqua); 216 Quantum Publishing (Caroline Dear); 219–221 Quantum Publishing (Marcos Bevilacqua).